AI
Self-Driving Cars
Materiality

Practical Advances in
Artificial Intelligence and Machine Learning

Dr. Lance B. Eliot, MBA, PhD

DEDICATION

To my incredible daughter, Lauren, and my incredible son, Michael.

Forest fortuna adiuvat (from the Latin; good fortune favors the brave).

CONTENTS

Acknowledgments iii

Introduction 1

Chapters

1 Eliot Framework for AI Self-Driving Cars 15

2 Baby Sea Lion and AI Self-Driving Cars 29

3 Traffic Lights and AI Self-Driving Cars 37

4 Roadway Edge Computing and AI Self-Driving Cars 45

5 Ground Penetrating Radar and AI Self-Driving Cars 59

6 Upstream Parable and AI Self-Driving Cars 71

7 Red-Light Auto-Stopping and Self-Driving Cars 87

8 Falseness of Superhuman AI Self-Driving Cars 103

9 Social Distancing and AI Self-Driving Cars 117

10 Apollo 13 Lessons and AI Self-Driving Cars 131

11 FutureLaw and AI Self-Driving Cars 145

Appendix A: Teaching with this Material 157

Other Self-Driving Car Books by This Author 165

About the Author 207

Addendum 208

Dr. Lance B. Eliot

ACKNOWLEDGMENTS

I have been the beneficiary of advice and counsel by many friends, colleagues, family, investors, and many others. I want to thank everyone that has aided me throughout my career. I write from the heart and the head, having experienced first-hand what it means to have others around you that support you during the good times and the tough times.

To Warren Bennis, one of my doctoral advisors and ultimately a colleague, I offer my deepest thanks and appreciation, especially for his calm and insightful wisdom and support.

To Mark Stevens and his generous efforts toward funding and supporting the USC Stevens Center for Innovation.

To Lloyd Greif and the USC Lloyd Greif Center for Entrepreneurial Studies for their ongoing encouragement of founders and entrepreneurs.

To Peter Drucker, William Wang, Aaron Levie, Peter Kim, Jon Kraft, Cindy Crawford, Jenny Ming, Steve Milligan, Chis Underwood, Frank Gehry, Buzz Aldrin, Steve Forbes, Bill Thompson, Dave Dillon, Alan Fuerstman, Larry Ellison, Jim Sinegal, John Sperling, Mark Stevenson, Anand Nallathambi, Thomas Barrack, Jr., and many other innovators and leaders that I have met and gained mightily from doing so.

Thanks to Ed Trainor, Kevin Anderson, James Hickey, Wendell Jones, Ken Harris, DuWayne Peterson, Mike Brown, Jim Thornton, Abhi Beniwal, Al Biland, John Nomura, Eliot Weinman, John Desmond, and many others for their unwavering support during my career.

And most of all thanks as always to Lauren and Michael, for their ongoing support and for having seen me writing and heard much of this material during the many months involved in writing it. To their patience and willingness to listen.

INTRODUCTION

This is a book that provides the newest innovations and the latest Artificial Intelligence (AI) advances about the emerging nature of AI-based autonomous self-driving driverless cars. Via recent advances in Artificial Intelligence (AI) and Machine Learning (ML), we are nearing the day when vehicles can control themselves and will not require and nor rely upon human intervention to perform their driving tasks (or, that <u>allow</u> for human intervention, but only *require* human intervention in very limited ways).

Similar to my other related books, which I describe in a moment and list the chapters in the Appendix A of this book, I am particularly focused on those advances that pertain to self-driving cars. The phrase "autonomous vehicles" is often used to refer to any kind of vehicle, whether it is ground-based or in the air or sea, and whether it is a cargo hauling trailer truck or a conventional passenger car. Though the aspects described in this book are certainly applicable to all kinds of autonomous vehicles, I am focused more so here on cars.

Indeed, I am especially known for my role in aiding the advancement of self-driving cars, serving currently as the Executive Director of the Cybernetic AI Self-Driving Cars Institute. In addition to writing software, designing and developing systems and software for self-driving cars, I also speak and write quite a bit about the topic. This book is a collection of some of my more advanced essays. For those of you that might have seen my essays posted elsewhere, I have updated them and integrated them into this book as one handy cohesive package.

You might be interested in companion books that I have written that provide additional key innovations and fundamentals about self-driving cars. Those books are entitled **"Introduction to Driverless Self-Driving Cars,"** **"Advances in AI and Autonomous Vehicles: Cybernetic Self-Driving Cars,"** **"Self-Driving Cars: "The Mother of All AI Projects,"** **"Innovation and Thought Leadership on Self-Driving Driverless Cars,"** **"New Advances in AI Autonomous Driverless Self-Driving Cars,"** **"Autonomous Vehicle Driverless Self-Driving Cars and Artificial Intelligence,"** **"Transformative Artificial Intelligence**

Driverless Self-Driving Cars," "Disruptive Artificial Intelligence and Driverless Self-Driving Cars, and "State-of-the-Art AI Driverless Self-Driving Cars," and "Top Trends in AI Self-Driving Cars," and "AI Innovations and Self-Driving Cars," "Crucial Advances for AI Driverless Cars," "Sociotechnical Insights and AI Driverless Cars," "Pioneering Advances for AI Driverless Cars" and "Leading Edge Trends for AI Driverless Cars," "The Cutting Edge of AI Autonomous Cars" and "The Next Wave of AI Self-Driving Cars" and "Revolutionary Innovations of AI Self-Driving Cars," and "AI Self-Driving Cars Breakthroughs," "Trailblazing Trends for AI Self-Driving Cars," "Ingenious Strides for AI Driverless Cars," "AI Self-Driving Cars Inventiveness," "Visionary Secrets of AI Driverless Cars," "Spearheading AI Self-Driving Cars," "Spurring AI Self-Driving Cars," "Avant-Garde AI Driverless Cars," "AI Self-Driving Cars Evolvement," "AI Driverless Cars Chrysalis," "Boosting AI Autonomous Cars," "AI Self-Driving Cars Trendsetting," "AI Autonomous Cars Forefront, "AI Autonomous Cars Emergence," "AI Autonomous Cars Progress," "AI Self-Driving Cars Prognosis," "AI Self-Driving Cars Momentum," "AI Self-Driving Cars Headway," "AI Self-Driving Cars Vicissitude," "AI Self-Driving Cars Autonomy," "AI Driverless Cars Transmutation," "AI Driverless Cars Potentiality," "AI Driverless Cars Realities," "AI Self-Driving Cars Materiality" (they are available on Amazon).

For this book, I am going to borrow my introduction from those companion books, since it does a good job of laying out the landscape of self-driving cars and my overall viewpoints on the topic.

INTRODUCTION TO SELF-DRIVING CARS

This is a book about self-driving cars. Someday in the future, we'll all have self-driving cars and this book will perhaps seem antiquated, but right now, we are at the forefront of the self-driving car wave. Daily news bombards us with flashes of new announcements by one car maker or another and leaves the impression that within the next few weeks or maybe months that the self-driving car will be here. A casual non-technical reader would assume from these news flashes that in fact we must be on the cusp of a true self-driving car. We are still quite a distance from having a true self-driving car.

A true self-driving car is akin to a moonshot. In the same manner that getting us to the moon was an incredible feat, likewise, is achieving a true self-driving car. Anybody that suggests or even brashly states that the true self-driving car is nearly here should be viewed with great skepticism. Indeed, you'll see that I often tend to use the word "hogwash" or "crock" when I assess much of the decidedly *fake news* about self-driving cars.

Indeed, I've been writing a popular blog post about self-driving cars and hitting hard on those that try to wave their hands and pretend that we are on the imminent verge of true self-driving cars. For many years, I've been known as the AI Insider. Besides writing about AI, I also develop AI software. I do what I describe. It also gives me insights into what others that are doing AI are really doing versus what it is said they are doing.

Many faithful readers had asked me to pull together my insightful short essays and put them into another book, which you are now holding.

For those of you that have been reading my essays over the years, this collection not only puts them together into one handy package, I also updated the essays and added new material. For those of you that are new to the topic of self-driving cars and AI, I hope you find these essays approachable and informative. I also tend to have a writing style with a bit of a voice, and so you'll see that I am times have a wry sense of humor and poke at conformity.

As a former professor and founder of an AI research lab, I for many years wrote in the formal language of academic writing. I published in referred journals and served as an editor for several AI journals. This writing here is not of the nature, and I have adopted a different and more informal style for these essays. That being said, I also do mention from time-to-time more rigorous material on AI and encourage you all to dig into those deeper and more formal materials if so interested.

I am also an AI practitioner. This means that I write AI software for a living. Currently, I head-up the Cybernetics Self-Driving Car Institute, where we are developing AI software for self-driving cars.

For those of you that are reading this book and have a penchant for writing code, you might consider taking a look at the open source code available for self-driving cars. This is a handy place to start learning how to develop AI for self-driving cars. There are also many new educational courses spring forth. There is a growing body of those wanting to learn about and develop self-driving cars, and a growing body of colleges, labs, and other avenues by which you can learn about self-driving cars.

This book will provide a foundation of aspects that I think will get you ready for those kinds of more advanced training opportunities. If you've already taken those classes, you'll likely find these essays especially interesting as they offer a perspective that I am betting few other instructors or faculty offered to you. These are challenging essays that ask you to think beyond the conventional about self-driving cars.

THE MOTHER OF ALL AI PROJECTS

In June 2017, Apple CEO Tim Cook came out and finally admitted that Apple has been working on a self-driving car. As you'll see in my essays, Apple was enmeshed in secrecy about their self-driving car efforts. We have only been able to read the tea leaves and guess at what Apple has been up to. The notion of an iCar has been floating for quite a while, and self-driving engineers and researchers have been signing tight-lipped Non-Disclosure Agreements (NDA's) to work on projects at Apple that were as shrouded in mystery as any military invasion plans might be.

Tim Cook said something that many others in the Artificial Intelligence (AI) field have been saying, namely, the creation of a self-driving car has got to be the mother of all AI projects. In other words, it is in fact a tremendous moonshot for AI. If a self-driving car can be crafted and the AI works as we hope, it means that we have made incredible strides with AI and that therefore it opens many other worlds of potential breakthrough accomplishments that AI can solve.

Is this hyperbole? Am I just trying to make AI seem like a miracle worker and so provide self-aggrandizing statements for those of us writing the AI software for self-driving cars? No, it is not hyperbole. Developing a true self-driving car is really, really, really hard to do. Let me take a moment to explain why. As a side note, I realize that the Apple CEO is known for at times uttering hyperbole, and he had previously said for example that the year 2012 was "the mother of all years," and he had said that the release of iOS 10 was "the mother of all releases" – all of which does suggest he likes to use the handy "mother of" expression. But, I assure you, in terms of true self-driving cars, he has hit the nail on the head. For sure.

When you think about a moonshot and how we got to the moon, there are some identifiable characteristics and those same aspects can be applied to creating a true self-driving car. You'll notice that I keep putting the word "true" in front of the self-driving car expression. I do so because as per my essay about the various levels of self-driving cars, there are some self-driving cars that are only somewhat of a self-driving car. The somewhat versions are ones that require a human driver to be ready to intervene. In my view, that's not a true self-driving car. A true self-driving car is one that requires no human driver intervention at all. It is a car that can entirely undertake via automation the driving task without any human driver needed. This is the essence of what is known as a Level 5 self-driving car. We are currently at the Level 2 and Level 3 mark, and not yet at Level 5.

Getting to the moon involved aspects such as having big stretch goals, incremental progress, experimentation, innovation, and so on. Let's review how this applied to the moonshot of the bygone era, and how it applies to the self-driving car moonshot of today.

Big Stretch Goal

Trying to take a human and deliver the human to the moon, and bring them back, safely, was an extremely large stretch goal at the time. No one knew whether it could be done. The technology wasn't available yet. The cost was huge. The determination would need to be fierce. Etc. To reach a Level 5 self-driving car is going to be the same. It is a big stretch goal. We can readily get to the Level 3, and we are able to see the Level 4 just up ahead, but a Level 5 is still an unknown as to if it is doable. It should eventually be doable and in the same way that we thought we'd eventually get to the moon, but when it will occur is a different story.

Incremental Progress

Getting to the moon did not happen overnight in one fell swoop. It took years and years of incremental progress to get there. Likewise for self-driving cars. Google has famously been striving to get to the Level 5, and pretty much been willing to forgo dealing with the intervening levels, but most of the other self-driving car makers are doing the incremental route. Let's get a good Level 2 and a somewhat Level 3 going. Then, let's improve the Level 3 and get a somewhat Level 4 going. Then, let's improve the Level 4 and finally arrive at a Level 5. This seems to be the prevalent way that we are going to achieve the true self-driving car.

Experimentation

You likely know that there were various experiments involved in perfecting the approach and technology to get to the moon. As per making incremental progress, we first tried to see if we could get a rocket to go into space and safety return, then put a monkey in there, then with a human, then we went all the way to the moon but didn't land, and finally we arrived at the mission that actually landed on the moon. Self-driving cars are the same way. We are doing simulations of self-driving cars. We do testing of self-driving cars on private land under controlled situations. We do testing of self-driving cars on public roadways, often having to meet regulatory requirements including for example having an engineer or equivalent in the car to take over the controls if needed. And so on. Experiments big and small are needed to figure out what works and what doesn't.

5

Innovation

There are already some advances in AI that are allowing us to progress toward self-driving cars. We are going to need even more advances. Innovation in all aspects of technology are going to be required to achieve a true self-driving car. By no means do we already have everything in-hand that we need to get there. Expect new inventions and new approaches, new algorithms, etc.

Setbacks

Most of the pundits are avoiding talking about potential setbacks in the progress toward self-driving cars. Getting to the moon involved many setbacks, some of which you never have heard of and were buried at the time so as to not dampen enthusiasm and funding for getting to the moon. A recurring theme in many of my included essays is that there are going to be setbacks as we try to arrive at a true self-driving car. Take a deep breath and be ready. I just hope the setbacks don't completely stop progress. I am sure that it will cause progress to alter in a manner that we've not yet seen in the self-driving car field. I liken the self-driving car of today to the excitement everyone had for Uber when it first got going. Today, we have a different view of Uber and with each passing day there are more regulations to the ride sharing business and more concerns raised. The darling child only stays a darling until finally that child acts up. It will happen the same with self-driving cars.

SELF-DRIVING CARS CHALLENGES

But what exactly makes things so hard to have a true self-driving car, you might be asking. You have seen cruise control for years and years. You've lately seen cars that can do parallel parking. You've seen YouTube videos of Tesla drivers that put their hands out the window as their car zooms along the highway, and seen to therefore be in a self-driving car. Aren't we just needing to put a few more sensors onto a car and then we'll have in-hand a true self-driving car? Nope.

Consider for a moment the nature of the driving task. We don't just let anyone at any age drive a car. Worldwide, most countries won't license a driver until the age of 18, though many do allow a learner's permit at the age of 15 or 16. Some suggest that a younger age would be physically too small to reach the controls of the car. Though this might be the case, we could easily adjust the controls to allow for younger aged and thus smaller stature.

It's not their physical size that matters. It's their cognitive development that matters.

To drive a car, you need to be able to reason about the car, what the car can and cannot do. You need to know how to operate the car. You need to know about how other cars on the road drive. You need to know what is allowed in driving such as speed limits and driving within marked lanes. You need to be able to react to situations and be able to avoid getting into accidents. You need to ascertain when to hit your brakes, when to steer clear of a pedestrian, and how to keep from ramming that motorcyclist that just cut you off.

Many of us had taken courses on driving. We studied about driving and took driver training. We had to take a test and pass it to be able to drive. The point being that though most adults take the driving task for granted, and we often "mindlessly" drive our cars, there is a significant amount of cognitive effort that goes into driving a car. After a while, it becomes second nature. You don't especially think about how you drive, you just do it. But, if you watch a novice driver, say a teenager learning to drive, you suddenly realize that there is a lot more complexity to it than we seem to realize.

Furthermore, driving is a very serious task. I recall when my daughter and son first learned to drive. They are both very conscientious people. They wanted to make sure that whatever they did, they did well, and that they did not harm anyone. Every day, when you get into a car, it is probably around 4,000 pounds of hefty metal and plastics (about two tons), and it is a lethal weapon. Think about it. You drive down the street in an object that weighs two tons and with the engine it can accelerate and ram into anything you want to hit. The damage a car can inflict is very scary. Both my children were surprised that they were being given the right to maneuver this monster of a beast that could cause tremendous harm entirely by merely letting go of the steering wheel for a moment or taking your eyes off the road.

In fact, in the United States alone there are about 30,000 deaths per year by auto accidents, which is around 100 per day. Given that there are about 263 million cars in the United States, I am actually more amazed that the number of fatalities is not a lot higher. During my morning commute, I look at all the thousands of cars on the freeway around me, and I think that if all of them decided to go zombie and drive in a crazy maniac way, there would be many people dead. Somehow, incredibly, each day, most people drive relatively safely. To me, that's a miracle right there. Getting millions and millions of people to be safe and sane when behind the wheel of a two ton mobile object, it's a feat that we as a society should admire with pride.

So, hopefully you are in agreement that the driving task requires a great deal of cognition. You don't' need to be especially smart to drive a car, and we've done quite a bit to make car driving viable for even the average dolt. There isn't an IQ test that you need to take to drive a car. If you can read and write, and pass a test, you pretty much can legally drive a car. There are of course some that drive a car and are not legally permitted to do so, plus there are private areas such as farms where drivers are young, but for public roadways in the United States, you can be generally of average intelligence (or less) and be able to legally drive.

This though makes it seem like the cognitive effort must not be much. If the cognitive effort was truly hard, wouldn't we only have Einstein's that could drive a car? We have made sure to keep the driving task as simple as we can, by making the controls easy and relatively standardized, and by having roads that are relatively standardized, and so on. It is as though Disneyland has put their Autopia into the real-world, by us all as a society agreeing that roads will be a certain way, and we'll all abide by the various rules of driving.

A modest cognitive task by a human is still something that stymies AI. You certainly know that AI has been able to beat chess players and be good at other kinds of games. This type of narrow cognition is not what car driving is about. Car driving is much wider. It requires knowledge about the world, which a chess playing AI system does not need to know. The cognitive aspects of driving are on the one hand seemingly simple, but at the same time require layer upon layer of knowledge about cars, people, roads, rules, and a myriad of other "common sense" aspects. We don't have any AI systems today that have that same kind of breadth and depth of awareness and knowledge.

As revealed in my essays, the self-driving car of today is using trickery to do particular tasks. It is all very narrow in operation. Plus, it currently assumes that a human driver is ready to intervene. It is like a child that we have taught to stack blocks, but we are needed to be right there in case the child stacks them too high and they begin to fall over. AI of today is brittle, it is narrow, and it does not approach the cognitive abilities of humans. This is why the true self-driving car is somewhere out in the future.

Another aspect to the driving task is that it is not solely a mind exercise. You do need to use your senses to drive. You use your eyes a vision sensors to see the road ahead. You vision capability is like a streaming video, which your brain needs to continually analyze as you drive. Where is the road? Is there a pedestrian in the way? Is there another car ahead of you? Your senses are relying a flood of info to your brain. Self-driving cars are trying to do the same, by using cameras, radar, ultrasound, and lasers. This is an attempt at mimicking how humans have senses and sensory apparatus.

Thus, the driving task is mental and physical. You use your senses, you use your arms and legs to manipulate the controls of the car, and you use your brain to assess the sensory info and direct your limbs to act upon the controls of the car. This all happens instantly. If you've ever perhaps gotten something in your eye and only had one eye available to drive with, you suddenly realize how dependent upon vision you are. If you have a broken foot with a cast, you suddenly realize how hard it is to control the brake pedal and the accelerator. If you've taken medication and your brain is maybe sluggish, you suddenly realize how much mental strain is required to drive a car.

An AI system that plays chess only needs to be focused on playing chess. The physical aspects aren't important because usually a human moves the chess pieces or the chessboard is shown on an electronic display. Using AI for a more life-and-death task such as analyzing MRI images of patients, this again does not require physical capabilities and instead is done by examining images of bits.

Driving a car is a true life-and-death task. It is a use of AI that can easily and at any moment produce death. For those colleagues of mine that are developing this AI, as am I, we need to keep in mind the somber aspects of this. We are producing software that will have in its virtual hands the lives of the occupants of the car, and the lives of those in other nearby cars, and the lives of nearby pedestrians, etc. Chess is not usually a life-or-death matter.

Driving is all around us. Cars are everywhere. Most of today's AI applications involve only a small number of people. Or, they are behind the scenes and we as humans have other recourse if the AI messes up. AI that is driving a car at 80 miles per hour on a highway had better not mess up. The consequences are grave. Multiply this by the number of cars, if we could put magically self-driving into every car in the USA, we'd have AI running in the 263 million cars. That's a lot of AI spread around. This is AI on a massive scale that we are not doing today and that offers both promise and potential peril.

There are some that want AI for self-driving cars because they envision a world without any car accidents. They envision a world in which there is no car congestion and all cars cooperate with each other. These are wonderful utopian visions.

They are also very misleading. The adoption of self-driving cars is going to be incremental and not overnight. We cannot economically just junk all existing cars. Nor are we going to be able to affordably retrofit existing cars. It is more likely that self-driving cars will be built into new cars and that over many years of gradual replacement of existing cars that we'll see the mix of self-driving cars become substantial in the real-world.

In these essays, I have tried to offer technological insights without being overly technical in my description, and also blended the business, societal, and economic aspects too. Technologists need to consider the non-technological impacts of what they do. Non-technologists should be aware of what is being developed.

We all need to work together to collectively be prepared for the enormous disruption and transformative aspects of true self-driving cars.

9

WHAT THIS BOOK PROVIDES

What does this book provide to you? It introduces many of the key elements about self-driving cars and does so with an AI based perspective. I weave together technical and non-technical aspects, readily going from being concerned about the cognitive capabilities of the driving task and how the technology is embodying this into self-driving cars, and in the next breath I discuss the societal and economic aspects.

They are all intertwined because that's the way reality is. You cannot separate out the technology per se, and instead must consider it within the milieu of what is being invented and innovated, and do so with a mindset towards the contemporary mores and culture that shape what we are doing and what we hope to do.

WHY THIS BOOK

I wrote this book to try and bring to the public view many aspects about self-driving cars that nobody seems to be discussing.

For business leaders that are either involved in making self-driving cars or that are going to leverage self-driving cars, I hope that this book will enlighten you as to the risks involved and ways in which you should be strategizing about how to deal with those risks.

For entrepreneurs, startups and other businesses that want to enter into the self-driving car market that is emerging, I hope this book sparks your interest in doing so, and provides some sense of what might be prudent to pursue.

For researchers that study self-driving cars, I hope this book spurs your interest in the risks and safety issues of self-driving cars, and also nudges you toward conducting research on those aspects.

For students in computer science or related disciplines, I hope this book will provide you with interesting and new ideas and material, for which you might conduct research or provide some career direction insights for you.

For AI companies and high-tech companies pursuing self-driving cars, this book will hopefully broaden your view beyond just the mere coding and development needed to make self-driving cars.

For all readers, I hope that you will find the material in this book to be stimulating. Some of it will be repetitive of things you already know. But I am pretty sure that you'll also find various eureka moments whereby you'll discover a new technique or approach that you had not earlier thought of. I am also betting that there will be material that forces you to rethink some of your current practices.

I am not saying you will suddenly have an epiphany and change what you are doing. I do think though that you will reconsider or perhaps revisit what you are doing.

For anyone choosing to use this book for teaching purposes, please take a look at my suggestions for doing so, as described in the Appendix. I have found the material handy in courses that I have taught, and likewise other faculty have told me that they have found the material handy, in some cases as extended readings and in other instances as a core part of their course (depending on the nature of the class).

In my writing for this book, I have tried carefully to blend both the practitioner and the academic styles of writing. It is not as dense as is typical academic journal writing, but at the same time offers depth by going into the nuances and trade-offs of various practices.

The word "deep" is in vogue today, meaning getting deeply into a subject or topic, and so is the word "unpack" which means to tease out the underlying aspects of a subject or topic. I have sought to offer material that addresses an issue or topic by going relatively deeply into it and make sure that it is well unpacked.

In any book about AI, it is difficult to use our everyday words without having some of them be misinterpreted. Specifically, it is easy to anthropomorphize AI. When I say that an AI system "knows" something, I do not want you to construe that the AI system has sentience and "knows" in the same way that humans do. They aren't that way, as yet. I have tried to use quotes around such words from time-to-time to emphasize that the words I am using should not be misinterpreted to ascribe true human intelligence to the AI systems that we know of today. If I used quotes around all such words, the book would be very difficult to read, and so I am doing so judiciously. Please keep that in mind as you read the material, thanks.

Some of the material is time-based in terms of covering underway activities, and though some of it might decay, nonetheless I believe you'll find the material useful and informative.

COMPANION BOOKS

1. **"Introduction to Driverless Self-Driving Cars"** by Dr. Lance Eliot
2. **"Innovation and Thought Leadership on Self-Driving Driverless Cars"** by Dr. Lance Eliot
3. **"Advances in AI and Autonomous Vehicles: Cybernetic Self-Driving Cars"** by Dr. Lance Eliot
4. **"Self-Driving Cars: The Mother of All AI Projects"** by Dr. Lance Eliot
5. **"New Advances in AI Autonomous Driverless Self-Driving Cars"** by Dr. Lance Eliot
6. **"Autonomous Vehicle Driverless Self-Driving Cars and Artificial Intelligence"** by Dr. Lance Eliot and Michael B. Eliot
7. **"Transformative Artificial Intelligence Driverless Self-Driving Cars"** by Dr. Lance Eliot
8. **"Disruptive Artificial Intelligence and Driverless Self-Driving Cars"** by Dr. Lance Eliot
9. "State-of-the-Art AI Driverless Self-Driving Cars" by Dr. Lance Eliot
10. "**Top Trends in AI Self-Driving Cars**" by Dr. Lance Eliot
11. **"AI Innovations and Self-Driving Cars"** by Dr. Lance Eliot
12. **"Crucial Advances for AI Driverless Cars"** by Dr. Lance Eliot
13. **"Sociotechnical Insights and AI Driverless Cars"** by Dr. Lance Eliot.
14. **"Pioneering Advances for AI Driverless Cars"** by Dr. Lance Eliot
15. **"Leading Edge Trends for AI Driverless Cars"** by Dr. Lance Eliot
16. **"The Cutting Edge of AI Autonomous Cars"** by Dr. Lance Eliot
17. **"The Next Wave of AI Self-Driving Cars"** by Dr. Lance Eliot
18. **"Revolutionary Innovations of AI Driverless Cars"** by Dr. Lance Eliot
19. **"AI Self-Driving Cars Breakthroughs"** by Dr. Lance Eliot
20. **"Trailblazing Trends for AI Self-Driving Cars"** by Dr. Lance Eliot
21. **"Ingenious Strides for AI Driverless Cars"** by Dr. Lance Eliot
22. **"AI Self-Driving Cars Inventiveness"** by Dr. Lance Eliot
23. **"Visionary Secrets of AI Driverless Cars"** by Dr. Lance Eliot
24. **"Spearheading AI Self-Driving Cars"** by Dr. Lance Eliot
25. **"Spurring AI Self-Driving Cars"** by Dr. Lance Eliot
26. **"Avant-Garde AI Driverless Cars"** by Dr. Lance Eliot
27. **"AI Self-Driving Cars Evolvement"** by Dr. Lance Eliot
28. **"AI Driverless Cars Chrysalis"** by Dr. Lance Eliot
29. **"Boosting AI Autonomous Cars"** by Dr. Lance Eliot
30. **"AI Self-Driving Cars Trendsetting"** by Dr. Lance Eliot
31. **"AI Autonomous Cars Forefront"** by Dr. Lance Eliot
32. **"AI Autonomous Cars Emergence"** by Dr. Lance Eliot
33. **"AI Autonomous Cars Progress"** by Dr. Lance Eliot
34. **"AI Self-Driving Cars Prognosis"** by Dr. Lance Eliot
35. **"AI Self-Driving Cars Momentum"** by Dr. Lance Eliot
36. **"AI Self-Driving Cars Headway"** by Dr. Lance Eliot
37. **"AI Self-Driving Cars Vicissitude"** by Dr. Lance Eliot
38. **"AI Self-Driving Cars Autonomy"** by Dr. Lance Eliot
39. **"AI Driverless Cars Transmutation"** by Dr. Lance Eliot
40. **"AI Driverless Cars Potentiality"** by Dr. Lance Eliot
41. **"AI Driverless Cars Realities"** by Dr. Lance Eliot
42. **"AI Self-Driving Cars Materiality"** by Dr. Lance Eliot

These books are available on Amazon and at other major global booksellers.

CHAPTER 1

ELIOT FRAMEWORK FOR AI SELF-DRIVING CARS

CHAPTER 1

ELIOT FRAMEWORK FOR
AI SELF-DRIVING CARS

This chapter is a core foundational aspect for understanding AI self-driving cars and I have used this same chapter in several of my other books to introduce the reader to essential elements of this field. Once you've read this chapter, you'll be prepared to read the rest of the material since the foundational essence of the components of autonomous AI driverless self-driving cars will have been established for you.

———————

When I give presentations about self-driving cars and teach classes on the topic, I have found it helpful to provide a framework around which the various key elements of self-driving cars can be understood and organized (see diagram at the end of this chapter). The framework needs to be simple enough to convey the overarching elements, but at the same time not so simple that it belies the true complexity of self-driving cars. As such, I am going to describe the framework here and try to offer in a thousand words (or more!) what the framework diagram itself intends to portray.

The core elements on the diagram are numbered for ease of reference. The numbering does not suggest any kind of prioritization of the elements. Each element is crucial. Each element has a purpose, and otherwise would not be included in the framework. For some self-driving cars, a particular element might be more important or somehow distinguished in comparison to other self-driving cars.

You could even use the framework to rate a particular self-driving car, doing so by gauging how well it performs in each of the elements of the framework. I will describe each of the elements, one at a time. After doing so, I'll discuss aspects that illustrate how the elements interact and perform during the overall effort of a self-driving car.

At the Cybernetic Self-Driving Car Institute, we use the framework to keep track of what we are working on, and how we are developing software that fills in what is needed to achieve Level 5 self-driving cars.

D-01: Sensor Capture

Let's start with the one element that often gets the most attention in the press about self-driving cars, namely, the sensory devices for a self-driving car.

On the framework, the box labeled as D-01 indicates "Sensor Capture" and refers to the processes of the self-driving car that involve collecting data from the myriad of sensors that are used for a self-driving car. The types of devices typically involved are listed, such as the use of mono cameras, stereo cameras, LIDAR devices, radar systems, ultrasonic devices, GPS, IMU, and so on.

These devices are tasked with obtaining data about the status of the self-driving car and the world around it. Some of the devices are continually providing updates, while others of the devices await an indication by the self-driving car that the device is supposed to collect data. The data might be first transformed in some fashion by the device itself, or it might instead be fed directly into the sensor capture as raw data. At that point, it might be up to the sensor capture processes to do transformations on the data. This all varies depending upon the nature of the devices being used and how the devices were designed and developed.

D-02: Sensor Fusion

Imagine that your eyeballs receive visual images, your nose receives odors, your ears receive sounds, and in essence each of your distinct sensory devices is getting some form of input. The input befits the nature of the device. Likewise, for a self-driving car, the cameras provide visual images, the radar returns radar reflections, and so on.

Each device provides the data as befits what the device does.

At some point, using the analogy to humans, you need to merge together what your eyes see, what your nose smells, what your ears hear, and piece it all together into a larger sense of what the world is all about and what is happening around you. Sensor fusion is the action of taking the singular aspects from each of the devices and putting them together into a larger puzzle.

Sensor fusion is a tough task. There are some devices that might not be working at the time of the sensor capture. Or, there might some devices that are unable to report well what they have detected. Again, using a human analogy, suppose you are in a dark room and so your eyes cannot see much. At that point, you might need to rely more so on your ears and what you hear. The same is true for a self-driving car. If the cameras are obscured due to snow and sleet, it might be that the radar can provide a greater indication of what the external conditions consist of.

In the case of a self-driving car, there can be a plethora of such sensory devices. Each is reporting what it can. Each might have its difficulties. Each might have its limitations, such as how far ahead it can detect an object. All of these limitations need to be considered during the sensor fusion task.

D-03: Virtual World Model

For humans, we presumably keep in our minds a model of the world around us when we are driving a car. In your mind, you know that the car is going at say 60 miles per hour and that you are on a freeway. You have a model in your mind that your car is surrounded by other cars, and that there are lanes to the freeway. Your model is not only based on what you can see, hear, etc., but also what you know about the nature of the world. You know that at any moment that car ahead of you can smash on its brakes, or the car behind you can ram into your car, or that the truck in the next lane might swerve into your lane.

The AI of the self-driving car needs to have a virtual world model, which it then keeps updated with whatever it is receiving from the sensor fusion, which received its input from the sensor capture and the sensory devices.

D-04: System Action Plan

By having a virtual world model, the AI of the self-driving car is able to keep track of where the car is and what is happening around the car. In addition, the AI needs to determine what to do next. Should the self-driving car hit its brakes? Should the self-driving car stay in its lane or swerve into the lane to the left? Should the self-driving car accelerate or slow down?

A system action plan needs to be prepared by the AI of the self-driving car. The action plan specifies what actions should be taken. The actions need to pertain to the status of the virtual world model. Plus, the actions need to be realizable.

This realizability means that the AI cannot just assert that the self-driving car should suddenly sprout wings and fly. Instead, the AI must be bound by whatever the self-driving car can actually do, such as coming to a halt in a distance of X feet at a speed of Y miles per hour, rather than perhaps asserting that the self-driving car come to a halt in 0 feet as though it could instantaneously come to a stop while it is in motion.

D-05: Controls Activation

The system action plan is implemented by activating the controls of the car to act according to what the plan stipulates. This might mean that the accelerator control is commanded to increase the speed of the car. Or, the steering control is commanded to turn the steering wheel 30 degrees to the left or right.

One question arises as to whether or not the controls respond as they are commanded to do. In other words, suppose the AI has commanded the accelerator to increase, but for some reason it does not do so. Or, maybe it tries to do so, but the speed of the car does not increase. The controls activation feeds back into the virtual world model, and simultaneously the virtual world model is getting updated from the sensors, the sensor capture, and the sensor fusion. This allows the AI to ascertain what has taken place as a result of the controls being commanded to take some kind of action.

By the way, please keep in mind that though the diagram seems to have a linear progression to it, the reality is that these are all aspects of the self-driving car that are happening in parallel and simultaneously. The sensors are capturing data, meanwhile the sensor fusion is taking place, meanwhile the virtual model is being updated, meanwhile the system action plan is being formulated and reformulated, meanwhile the controls are being activated.

This is the same as a human being that is driving a car. They are eyeballing the road, meanwhile they are fusing in their mind the sights, sounds, etc., meanwhile their mind is updating their model of the world around them, meanwhile they are formulating an action plan of what to do, and meanwhile they are pushing their foot onto the pedals and steering the car. In the normal course of driving a car, you are doing all of these at once. I mention this so that when you look at the diagram, you will think of the boxes as processes that are all happening at the same time, and not as though only one happens and then the next.

They are shown diagrammatically in a simplistic manner to help comprehend what is taking place. You though should also realize that they are working in parallel and simultaneous with each other. This is a tough aspect in that the inter-element communications involve latency and other aspects that must be taken into account. There can be delays in one element updating and then sharing its latest status with other elements.

D-06: Automobile & CAN

Contemporary cars use various automotive electronics and a Controller Area Network (CAN) to serve as the components that underlie the driving aspects of a car. There are Electronic Control Units (ECU's) which control subsystems of the car, such as the engine, the brakes, the doors, the windows, and so on.

The elements D-01, D-02, D-03, D-04, D-05 are layered on top of the D-06, and must be aware of the nature of what the D-06 is able to do and not do.

D-07: In-Car Commands

Humans are going to be occupants in self-driving cars. In a Level 5 self-driving car, there must be some form of communication that takes place between the humans and the self-driving car. For example, I go into a self-driving car and tell it that I want to be driven over to Disneyland, and along the way I want to stop at In-and-Out Burger. The self-driving car now parses what I've said and tries to then establish a means to carry out my wishes.

In-car commands can happen at any time during a driving journey. Though my example was about an in-car command when I first got into my self-driving car, it could be that while the self-driving car is carrying out the journey that I change my mind. Perhaps after getting stuck in traffic, I tell the self-driving car to forget about getting the burgers and just head straight over to the theme park. The self-driving car needs to be alert to in-car commands throughout the journey.

D-08: V2X Communications

We will ultimately have self-driving cars communicating with each other, doing so via V2V (Vehicle-to-Vehicle) communications. We will also have self-driving cars that communicate with the roadways and other aspects of the transportation infrastructure, doing so via V2I (Vehicle-to-Infrastructure).

The variety of ways in which a self-driving car will be communicating with other cars and infrastructure is being called V2X, whereby the letter X means whatever else we identify as something that a car should or would want to communicate with. The V2X communications will be taking place simultaneous with everything else on the diagram, and those other elements will need to incorporate whatever it gleans from those V2X communications.

D-09: Deep Learning

The use of Deep Learning permeates all other aspects of the self-driving car. The AI of the self-driving car will be using deep learning to do a better job at the systems action plan, and at the controls activation, and at the sensor fusion, and so on.

Currently, the use of artificial neural networks is the most prevalent form of deep learning. Based on large swaths of data, the neural networks attempt to "learn" from the data and therefore direct the efforts of the self-driving car accordingly.

D-10: Tactical AI

Tactical AI is the element of dealing with the moment-to-moment driving of the self-driving car. Is the self-driving car staying in its lane of the freeway? Is the car responding appropriately to the controls commands? Are the sensory devices working?

For human drivers, the tactical equivalent can be seen when you watch a novice driver such as a teenager that is first driving. They are focused on the mechanics of the driving task, keeping their eye on the road while also trying to properly control the car.

D-11: Strategic AI

The Strategic AI aspects of a self-driving car are dealing with the larger picture of what the self-driving car is trying to do. If I had asked that the self-driving car take me to Disneyland, there is an overall journey map that needs to be kept and maintained.

There is an interaction between the Strategic AI and the Tactical AI. The Strategic AI is wanting to keep on the mission of the driving, while the Tactical AI is focused on the particulars underway in the driving effort. If the Tactical AI seems to wander away from the overarching mission, the Strategic AI wants to see why and get things back on track. If the Tactical AI realizes that there is something amiss on the self-driving car, it needs to alert the Strategic AI accordingly and have an adjustment to the overarching mission that is underway.

D-12: Self-Aware AI

Very few of the self-driving cars being developed are including a Self-Aware AI element, which we at the Cybernetic Self-Driving Car Institute believe is crucial to Level 5 self-driving cars.

The Self-Aware AI element is intended to watch over itself, in the sense that the AI is making sure that the AI is working as intended. Suppose you had a human driving a car, and they were starting to drive erratically. Hopefully, their own self-awareness would make them realize they themselves are driving poorly, such as perhaps starting to fall asleep after having been driving for hours on end. If you had a passenger in the car, they might be able to alert the driver if the driver is starting to do something amiss. This is exactly what the Self-Aware

AI element tries to do, it becomes the overseer of the AI, and tries to detect when the AI has become faulty or confused, and then find ways to overcome the issue.

D-13: Economic

The economic aspects of a self-driving car are not per se a technology aspect of a self-driving car, but the economics do indeed impact the nature of a self-driving car. For example, the cost of outfitting a self-driving car with every kind of possible sensory device is prohibitive, and so choices need to be made about which devices are used. And, for those sensory devices chosen, whether they would have a full set of features or a more limited set of features.

We are going to have self-driving cars that are at the low-end of a consumer cost point, and others at the high-end of a consumer cost point. You cannot expect that the self-driving car at the low-end is going to be as robust as the one at the high-end. I realize that many of the self-driving car pundits are acting as though all self-driving cars will be the same, but they won't be. Just like anything else, we are going to have self-driving cars that have a range of capabilities. Some will be better than others. Some will be safer than others. This is the way of the real-world, and so we need to be thinking about the economics aspects when considering the nature of self-driving cars.

D-14: Societal

This component encompasses the societal aspects of AI which also impacts the technology of self-driving cars. For example, the famous Trolley Problem involves what choices should a self-driving car make when faced with life-and-death matters. If the self-driving car is about to either hit a child standing in the roadway, or instead ram into a tree at the side of the road and possibly kill the humans in the self-driving car, which choice should be made?

We need to keep in mind the societal aspects will underlie the AI of the self-driving car. Whether we are aware of it explicitly or not, the AI will have embedded into it various societal assumptions.

D-15: Innovation

I included the notion of innovation into the framework because we can anticipate that whatever a self-driving car consists of, it will continue to be innovated over time. The self-driving cars coming out in the next several years will undoubtedly be different and less innovative than the versions that come out in ten years hence, and so on.

Framework Overall

For those of you that want to learn about self-driving cars, you can potentially pick a particular element and become specialized in that aspect. Some engineers are focusing on the sensory devices. Some engineers focus on the controls activation. And so on. There are specialties in each of the elements.

Researchers are likewise specializing in various aspects. For example, there are researchers that are using Deep Learning to see how best it can be used for sensor fusion. There are other researchers that are using Deep Learning to derive good System Action Plans. Some are studying how to develop AI for the Strategic aspects of the driving task, while others are focused on the Tactical aspects.

A well-prepared all-around software developer that is involved in self-driving cars should be familiar with all of the elements, at least to the degree that they know what each element does. This is important since whatever piece of the pie that the software developer works on, they need to be knowledgeable about what the other elements are doing.

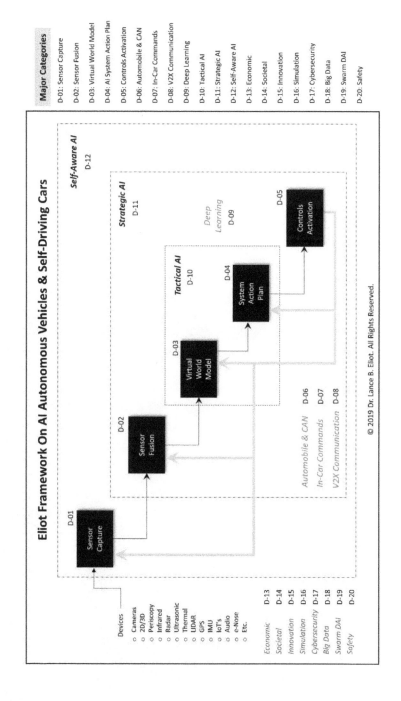

Eliot Framework On AI Autonomous Vehicles & Self-Driving Cars

Major Categories

D-01: Sensor Capture
D-02: Sensor Fusion
D-03: Virtual World Model
D-04: AI System Action Plan
D-05: Controls Activation
D-06: Automobile & CAN
D-07: In-Car Commands
D-08: V2X Communication
D-09: Deep Learning
D-10: Tactical AI
D-11: Strategic AI
D-12: Self-Aware AI
D-13: Economic
D-14: Societal
D-15: Innovation
D-16: Simulation
D-17: Cybersecurity
D-18: Big Data
D-19: Swarm DAI
D-20: Safety

CHAPTER 2
BABY SEA LION
AND
AI SELF-DRIVING CARS

CHAPTER 2

BABY SEA LION
AND AI SELF-DRIVING CARS

There was a bit of extra excitement recently in the San Francisco Bay Area traffic when a baby sea lion decided it was time to checkout rush hour activities and so wandered or waddled onto the hectic and perilous Highway 101. In case you aren't familiar with California drivers and their predilections, they are famous for a stern take-no-prisoners brashness when it comes to dealing with rush hour conflagrations.

Dare anything or anybody get into their way, which worsens an already worst-case clog that accompanies the dreadful rush hour traffic, you'll see hotheaded road rage acts and oftentimes bizarre attempts to push or squeeze their way around traffic using emergency lanes and whatever else might be within reach, illegal or endangering, many don't care.

What happened to the doe-eyed innocent wanderer that was merely curious about all the hubbub on the byway?

Thankfully, in a moment of unplanned humanity, some drivers purposely blocked traffic so that the sea lion pup would not get runover, and others got out of their cars to shoo the intruder over to the side of the road. It gives one hope for the world and our survival overall on this planet.

Apparently, one enterprising good Samaritan used a handkerchief, waving it seemingly like you might at the Pamplona bull run, hoping it would inspire the wayward mammal into getting out of harm's way. Ultimately, a California Highway Patrol (CHP) car showed-up and the officers did more than just try to herd the creature off the busy road, they opened the backdoor of their patrol car and the pup leaped right into the backseat, not needing a baton or handcuffs as inducements.

The sea lion then got a free ride to the local animal humane society, which though the journey didn't also get the mammal the archetypal sirens and flashing lights treatment, at least he was able to get some rest and relaxation after what must have been a quite harrowing experience. Just think of the stories he had to tell when he eventually got back with the colony or raft that he came from. Maybe the other sea lions wouldn't even believe the story and assume that it is yet another tall tale by a young pup with a vivid imagination.

Here's an interesting question for you.

What would a self-driving driverless autonomous car have done?

In other words, suppose that rather than the traffic being composed of human driven cars, instead it was a slew of autonomous cars. Would the autonomous cars realize the nature of the situation, or might they just keep on rolling along?

It's instructive to consider such a use case and reveals insights about the design and development of self-driving driverless cars.

Edge Cases For Autonomous Cars

Some pundits might decry the situation as a once-in-blue-moon circumstance and therefore it is not of importance or considered of any notable consequence to study. This is no more than an edge or corner case, they say, meaning that it is rare and therefore not something to be dealing with now. Let driverless cars first become proficient on everyday driving aspects, and later on come back to the oddball instances, they assert.

How many times will any of us ever experience a sea lion on a busy roadway? Admittedly, likely close to never, but then again you can logically and readily generalize the act of the sea lion to some other kind of animal. The news is replete with stories of animals entering our streets and highways in the midst of car traffic, including touching tales about ducks doing so, bears doing so, crocodiles doing so, and of course the everyday dogs and cats that are ubiquitous in our society.

If you are willing to agree that the sea lion is emblematic of a much larger set of possibilities, this hopefully is persuasive that perhaps this instance is not akin to a meteor striking earth or some other one-in-a-million chance of happening. The odds seem high enough, along with the sad and dire consequence to the meddlesome animal if it were to get runover, we should feel emboldened to argue that emerging autonomous cars ought to be prepared to deal with this type of situation.

Idealized Futuristic Handling By Autonomous Cars

In theory, eventually, we'll have autonomous cars that are interconnected with each other, doing so via V2V (vehicle-to-vehicle) electronic communications. The value of having V2V is that the self-driving cars will be able to share roadway status and provide cautions and insights to each other. Maybe there is a sofa that fell onto the freeway and the first autonomous car that spots it would quickly broadcast to any nearby driverless cars to be wary of the debris in the roadway.

For the case of the sea lion, presumably whichever autonomous car was the first to spot the wanderer, the AI using V2V would beam out a warning to the rest of traffic. Once the warning was received, the other driverless cars could at least hopefully opt to slowdown as they approached the location of the sea lion.

Would the AI of an autonomous car also determine that it would make sense to stop the driverless car and block other traffic?

You might say that there would be no need to do so, assuming that all other traffic has gotten the V2V messaging. But, it is possible that some of the other driverless cars might not have gotten the electronic message, and if there are also any human driven cars in the mix, perhaps not equipped with the V2V, acting to block the road to protect the animal might be sensible to contend with any loopholes.

In a twist that might surprise you, would the human passenger inside an autonomous car be able to possibly override the self-driving car in terms of the AI deciding to bring the driverless car to a halt?

Let's first consider the other side of that coin, namely what about a human passenger urging the autonomous car to come to a stop.

Consider that maybe a human passenger inside a driverless car might see the sea lion, possibly doing so before the sensors of an autonomous car did, and the human passenger might urge the AI to stop the car and block the road. This though is somewhat problematic, because suppose the human passenger uttered such a command and yet there wasn't any bona fide reason for the driverless car to come to a stop in the middle of traffic? The human could be drunk, they could be mistaken, they could be plain crazy, etc.

Do we want AI systems that blindly accept whatever the human passenger tells them to do?

This brings us back to my other question, the one dealing with the notion that a human passenger might command the AI to not stop the self-driving car, in spite of a sea lion having been detected by the autonomous car. You might instantly be angry that any human could be so uncaring, but suppose they were urgently trying to get to a hospital for themselves or had some other high priority need.

How is the AI to decide which is right, whether its own programmed automation is "right" to stop for the sea lion, or whether the human passenger is "right" to keep going, presumably attempting to avoid hitting the sea lion and yet not helping to especially protect or save the sea lion.

Do not be fooled by whatever exaggerated claims you might read about in the mass media and assume that the AI of autonomous cars will have human-like common sense reasoning, they certainly won't right away, and it is an ongoing debate as to when if ever they might be so armed.

Conclusion

I've brought up the story of the meandering sea lion to illuminate an even larger topic overall. The advent of autonomous cars means that we will now have non-human drivers, essentially AI systems, potentially making human-like choices while undertaking the driving task. Today, we assume that the human driver will take appropriate action and be held accountable when they don't.

This is a serious and unresolved matter for self-driving cars. The ethical questions abound when it comes to the choices to be made when driving a car. Oftentimes referred to as the Trolley Problem, a philosophical thought experiment about having to make hard life-or-death choices, the automakers and tech firms are currently without any specific guidance on what autonomous cars are supposed to do in these situations.

As a society, we'll need to find some amenable means to figure out the manner in which these AI driven driverless cars will make key societal decisions that impact us all, doing so in real-time, in the moment that something arises, including those instances involving endearing and innocent waddling baby sea lions that decide to cross the road.

CHAPTER 3
TRAFFIC LIGHTS
AND
AI SELF-DRIVING CARS

CHAPTER 3

TRAFFIC LIGHTS
AND
AI SELF-DRIVING CARS

It is a bit of a miracle that each day we drive around and encounter traffic signals that by the mere act of shining a light of differing colors gets us to all come to a peaceful stop, wait for one another to proceed, and then continue along on our own merry way.

The magic of red, yellow, green.

A red light though does not have some kind of laser beam that will zap any cars that decide to not come to a proper stop.

There isn't a hidden steel mesh that might suddenly pop-up from beneath the street to prevent cars from running a red light.

Instead, we stop at a red light because we are supposed to do so. Sure, you have the potential for getting a moving violation ticket if you don't abide by the red light, which I'm sure reins in most of us, and there is also the danger of getting rammed by a car rightfully coming through the intersection, so we presumably do calculate our life-or-death chances and generally stop at red lights by weighing the risks of running a red.

All in all, it's an amazing sight to see, namely the 225 million licensed drivers in the United States generally agreeing to accept and be managed by traffic signals. I dare say it would be nearly impossible to get that many people to agree to any particular thing of any kind, yet by-and-large we all do agree when it comes to obeying traffic lights (most of the time).

Sadly, not everyone always does abide, and there is a significant portion of the annual 6.3M car crashes and 37,000 annual car-related deaths that can be attributed to violating a red light. Some violators do so out of a miscalculation, some do so because they didn't see the red, some are drunk, some are car racing, some believe they are more important than the rest of us, and so on. Lots of reasons, but the end result can be disastrous.

Estimates are that there are 300,000 traffic signals across America.

I am pretty sure that a disproportionate share seems to be on the streets that I use to get to work. There is nothing more frustrating than getting stuck at one red light after another, seemingly as though they are in cahoots with each other and wanting to keep me from getting to work on time. Admittedly, I try to get out of the red light abyss by purposely speeding up to try and catch the green light up ahead, but it often requires going so excessively above the speed limit that I cave in and drop my quest (though other audacious speeders near me seem to not care).

One interesting stat that often is quoted suggests that we spend perhaps 6 months of our lives sitting at red lights. I've not added-up my red-light waiting times to see whether this stat is applicable. Given the at times unbearable on-hold at red lights I've endured, intuitively it sure seems like the grand total over a driving lifetime could be 6 months, or maybe it is more like 6 years where I live.

Traffic signals have evolved over time.

Plus, different countries have used differing colors or shapes for their traffic signals.

Since displaying only a color could be misinterpreted if you are color blind, there are traffic signals that also use shapes to distinguish the colors. Some traffic lights use a kind of emoticon etched onto the lenses as a means to distinguish the colors. In some places, blue is used as a color, while others use orange as a color for their traffic lights. You can use sounds for each of the colors, and you can make the lights flash or not flash, be bright or be dull, be stacked vertically or be shown horizontally, etc.

Here's a claim that's been making the rounds, once we have self-driving driverless autonomous car there won't be a need for traffic signals, and they'll all be quietly removed and turned into scrap.

Let's unpack the claim.

Why Traffic Signals Will Become Extinct

You might be wondering why pundits are asserting that the emergence of driverless cars will lead to the extinction of traffic signals.

The logic is that driverless cars are going to have V2V (vehicle-to-vehicle) electronic communications, allowing each autonomous car to electronically network with their brethren self-driving cars. When one self-driving car approaches an intersection, it will politely alert any cars coming toward the intersection to be aware of their upcoming passage through the intersection.

In theory, each driverless car will time its own approach to the intersection to allow other driverless cars to pass safely through the intersection.

Imagine that you and I were driving our own cars and had agreed to speak on our respective cell phones as we approached an intersection from different sides. I might tell you that in three seconds I'll be into the intersection, and so you realize that you need to slow down to allow my passage, and then after I've cleared the intersection you proceed through it. The driverless cars are able to do the same, via electronic communication, in split seconds worth of timing.

Multiply this kind of civility by the dozens of driverless cars that approach the intersection, or ultimately the thousands upon thousands that would pass through any busy city intersection on any given hour or any given day. All of them would be programmed to be courteous to each other, doing so to avoid hitting each other.

Simulations trying to show the efficacy of this are pretty neat to watch. Simulated cars streaming toward intersections, and potential certain death, which nonetheless suddenly shift and tweak their driving to ensure none get hit and yet they all eventually get through the intersection. I doubt that a horde of ants could do as well.

In this federated autonomous dance, a traffic signal has no place, it is superfluous. Indeed, a conventional traffic signal probably could not do what the simulation is doing, since the faked cars are not waiting necessarily altogether and instead are each passing forward as they can, somewhat like the maneuvering of cars at a roundabout or traffic circle.

Might as well start hauling all those 300,000 traffic signals to the scrapyard.

Traffic Signal Not Quite So Dead After All

As Mark Twain might say, please don't be so fast to write an obituary for traffic signals.

First, there are going to be for many years an ongoing mixture of human driven cars and driverless cars.

There are about 250 million conventional cars in the United States alone and those are not going to suddenly disappear when autonomous cars arise. We don't even know if human driving will ever be cut-off or denied, though there are driverless car advocates that argue vehemently to get human driving expunged right away.

If there are human drivers, it likely makes sense to keep the traffic signals in place.

That being said, we might transform the nature of the traffic signal.

Rather than the signal being a set of lights, perhaps the traffic signal is converted over into an electronic beacon that sends out a non-visible indication of the red, yellow, and green status. Human drivers will then be required to have in their cars a piece of relatively simple automation that would detect the electronic signal and let the human driver know the status of the traffic indictor.

As such, the traffic signal wouldn't even need to be placed into the middle of an intersection anymore. It could be on a nearby wall or building, or possibly be a "black box" emitting device bolted to a pole or fire hydrant. The signaling device could be much smaller than a normal traffic signal and be less likely to wear out (lightbulbs in traffic signals constitute a fair amount of maintenance effort).

Overall, it is anticipated that our roadway infrastructure is going to gradually be equipped with devices that can communicate to via V2I (vehicle-to-infrastructure) electronic communications. For driverless cars, they will get V2I electronic messages from bridges that are closed, from streets that are being repaired, from tollways that specify the cost to cross, and driverless cars will be able to interact with the infrastructure around them as needed.

Though this handy V2I arrangement will be feasible (once it's put in place, at a substantial cost, mind you), let's not forget about the other people that rely upon traffic signals. Pedestrians look at traffic signals. Bicyclists look at traffic signals. Motorcyclists look at traffic signals. And so on.

The use of lights is a pretty convenient form of communication. If the only emitting signal is electronic, you'd need to have a device on you or with you to detect it. Lights that are red, green, or yellow are readily seen and readily understood, not needing any added hardware or encumbrance.

Rather than junking traffic signals, it would seem more likely that we would gradually augment existing traffic signals with electronic beacons, which is already being done for various smart city efforts, and have a dual mode of communication, both the use of lights and the use of V2V and V2I.

Conclusion

There is the old joke about the person visiting a town and being driven in a car by a local. The local comes up to a red light and darts through it. The visitor is shaken and puzzled. Upon arriving at another red light, once again the local zooms through the red. Then, oddly, the local hits the brakes upon coming up to a green light.

Clearing his throat, the visitor asks why in the world did the driver opt to run the reds and now come to a halt at a green light. The driver turns to the visitor and explains, well, because my brother might be coming the other way.

Traffic signals are obeyed by a voluntary form of conditioning. Whether driverless cars will do better than humans, assuming that someday there are only autonomous cars on the roadways, remains to be seen. Yes, the self-driving cars won't get drunk and won't presumably try to road race, yet there is still the chances of system errors, glitches, and even cyber hacks that could undermine any kind of perfection in such matters.

I suppose though that by the time we have achieved an all autonomous cars era, we'll probably have flying cars by then, in which case, traffic signals might become extinct since we won't be on the ground anymore anyway.

CHAPTER 4

ROADWAY EDGE COMPUTING AND AI SELF-DRIVING CARS

CHAPTER 4

ROADWAY EDGE COMPUTING

AND

AI SELF-DRIVING CARS

Have you ever been driving a car and found yourself reaching an exasperating sensory overload in the act of driving the vehicle?

This can happen.

Suppose you are driving your car in the rain, which right away ups the ante for performing the driving task.

With rain slickened streets and a massive downpour obscuring your view of the traffic ahead, the odds are that you are having to strain to keep the car from slipping and sliding and are mightily seeking to avoid hitting any nearby vehicles or pedestrians.

Pretend that you have your family in the car with you, along with some out-of-town guests that you are toting around, and your beloved family pet is squeezed in there too, a golden retriever that loves to go for car rides.

At any moment in time, one or more family members might be telling you to watch out for a big semi-trailer truck that is within inches of your car in the lane to your right. And, the guests you are hosting might be pointing out that you need to go slower and be more mindful of large puddles of water on the roadway.

Even your beloved dog gets into the act, barking every time that you make a sudden maneuver to avert a car crash due to other maniac drivers that are recklessly driving in the rain.

You, the driver of the car, must remain steadfast in driving the car, and somehow also receive these varied inputs from your car mates, ascertaining whether they are providing you with helpful info to ensure a safe drive, or maybe providing only verbal clutter that distracts from you from performing the arduous driving chore.

There's a ton of verbal messaging flying through the air in that car, making for a large amount of sensory input to be processed.

Plus, you are visually scanning the roadway, mentally processing the myriad of elements in the rainy environment.

Is that car to your left going to veer into your lane, perhaps doing so since they might not have a clear view of the traffic as a result of their rain-soaked side mirrors?

That pedestrian on the sidewalk appears to be poised to dart across the street, jaywalking, opting to get out of the rain quickly rather than doing the right thing and walking down to the proper crosswalk at the corner.

You've got your eyes on the signal at the next intersection, currently showing a green light but it might soon switch to yellow and then red.

Would it be better to gun it and try to make the green, squeaking into the intersection if the light goes to yellow and then red, or would it be safer to start slowing down in anticipation of the red light that will soon inevitably appear?

Maybe the car behind you will try to rush-up upon your car, wanting to make it before the green light becomes the red light, and if you opt to slow down the other car might ram into your car.

Meanwhile, your "teammates" inside the car are all offering sage advice, some saying that you can make the green light by hammering down on the gas pedal, while others are urging you to get ready to halt at the intersection and are bracing for a sudden stop.

The golden retriever is offering his two cents too, whimpering about something, maybe over the green light versus red light dilemma, or it could be that he sees a stick outside the car and wants you to let him out of the car to go retrieve it.

Yikes!

A lot is going on.

Sensory Overload In Car Driving

Upon contemplating how often these kinds of sensory overload situations seem to arise, it is nearly a miracle that we don't have more car accidents than we already do.

Whenever you get into your car and head out into traffic, the amount of info you'll be getting during the course of a driving journey can range from being relatively modest to becoming a humungous deluge.

There's essential info such as the status of a traffic signal, along with numerous flashing signs that might be warning you to watch out for a flooded street or imploring you to slow down.

Other nearby cars are also a kind of signal or info that you are receiving since the behavior of those other cars and their drivers will shape where you can go and what you need to watch out for.

And, there are those pesky but treasured passengers, acting like back-seat drivers and inundating you with driving advice.

Speaking of driving advice, teenage novice drivers often find that they are unable to cope with an excessive amount of input when first learning to drive.

Astute parents discover that trying to aid their teenage novice driver by bombarding them with instructions when initially driving can be overwhelming and do more harm than good. You gradually realize that it is best to offer key points at key junctures, such as watch out for that double-parked van, rather than continually blathering about every minuscule detail of the driving task.

When we have true self-driving cars, the AI of the driverless car will be programmed to cope with complex driving situations and be able to presumably handle whatever volume of inputs comes it's way.

There is a bit of cheating going on right now in that most of the existing tryouts of self-driving cars do not engage the human passengers in a dialogue about the driving task. Thus, the AI doesn't have to deal as yet with vocal and insistent occupants that are offering varied opinions about which way to go or how to best drive the car.

Some believe that the automakers and self-driving tech firms won't ever aim to allow occupants to offer driving tips and comments, though I've pointed out that this is something that humans are going to want to do and pretending to avoid the matter is like burying your head in the sand.

Here's an interesting question to consider: *Should we be worried about true self-driving cars being potentially overloaded with sensory inputs akin to how humans can get overloaded?*

Yes, it's a valid concern.

One aspect that few are yet discussing involves an overload of V2X (vehicle-to-everything) electronic communications.

Let's unpack the matter and find out what it's about.

The Levels Of Self-Driving Cars

It is important to clarify what I mean when referring to true self-driving cars.

True self-driving cars are ones that the AI drives the car entirely on its own and there isn't any human assistance during the driving task.

These driverless vehicles are considered a Level 4 and Level 5, while a car that requires a human driver to co-share the driving effort is usually considered at a Level 2 or Level 3. The cars that co-share the driving task are described as being semi-autonomous, and typically contain a variety of automated add-on's that are referred to as ADAS (Advanced Driver-Assistance Systems).

There is not yet a true self-driving car at Level 5, which we don't yet even know if this will be possible to achieve, and nor how long it will take to get there.

Meanwhile, the Level 4 efforts are gradually trying to get some traction by undergoing very narrow and selective public roadway trials, though there is controversy over whether this testing should be allowed per se (we are all life-or-death guinea pigs in an experiment taking place on our highways and byways, some point out).

Since semi-autonomous cars require a human driver, the adoption of those types of cars won't be markedly different than driving conventional vehicles, so I'm not going to include them in this discussion about sensory overload (though for clarification, Level 2 and Level 3 could indeed have sensory overload impact their systems and thus this discussion overall is relevant even to semi-autonomous cars).

For semi-autonomous cars, it is equally important that I mention a disturbing aspect that's been arising, namely that in spite of those human drivers that keep posting videos of themselves falling asleep at the wheel of a Level 2 or Level 3 car, we all need to avoid being misled into believing that the driver can take away their attention from the driving task while driving a semi-autonomous car.

You are the responsible party for the driving actions of the vehicle, regardless of how much automation might be tossed into a Level 2 or Level 3.

Self-Driving Cars And Update Problem

For Level 4 and Level 5 true self-driving vehicles, there won't be a human driver involved in the driving task.

All occupants will be passengers.

The AI is doing the driving.

One aspect that will be a boon to driverless cars is the advent of V2X electronic communications, which refers to the notion that the AI of the self-driving car will be able to receive and send electronic messages to other roadway-related entities.

There will be V2V (vehicle-to-vehicle) electronic transmissions, allowing a driverless car to send out messages to other nearby driverless cars (this is considered one type of V2X capability).

Imagine that a driverless car has encountered debris in the roadway and can quickly let other self-driving cars behind it know that there's say a couch that's plopped onto the fast lane.

By using V2V, the AI of the driverless car that first spots the offending debris can spread the word to other self-driving cars. As a result, those other self-driving cars might opt to slow down or get out of the fast lane before they come upon the debris or exit early from the highway and avoid the blocked lane entirely.

Prevailing standards indicate that V2V uses a Wifi-like broadcast capability with a range of about 300 meters, suggesting that if a driverless car transmits a V2V message to other driverless cars nearby, those, in turn, could aid in spreading the message by sending it along to other self-driving cars and in approximately 5 to 7 hops get the message to vehicles nearly a mile away.

I refer to this as enabling a potential form of automotive omnipresence, allowing any given driverless car to essentially piece together a bigger picture of what's going on nearby, far beyond the normal limits of everyday vision and radar.

There will also be V2I (vehicle-to-infrastructure) electronic communications, yet another type of V2X.

We'll eventually have our roadway infrastructure wired-up with computers that can electronically give their status. A bridge that's out of commission can use V2I to let any approaching driverless cars and trucks know that the bridge is closed to traffic.

Some believe we'll also have V2P (vehicle-to-pedestrian) capabilities.

A pedestrian using their smartphone will be able to send a signal to self-driving cars coming down a street, telling those driverless cars that the pedestrian is intending to cross the street. This heads-up would be intended to reduce the chances that a pedestrian might be otherwise undetected and get hit by a driverless car.

Let's focus on V2V.

At first thought, the idea of having other nearby cars let you know about local driving conditions seems to be a godsend.

Human drivers have to guess about roadway issues by spotting clues such as cars ahead that are all slowing down, perhaps due to debris in the lane, though it could be some other problem altogether that is causing the cars to hit their brakes.

Just imagine if all human drivers were equipped with walkie-talkies and could yell out whatever they spot while driving, providing a boatload of added driving info to other nearby drivers.

Sure, today there are social media-oriented platforms that allow human drivers to indicate limited amounts of roadway conditions, which then get displayed on GPS maps for others to see, but that's a teensy tiny kind of notification in comparison to what V2V promises.

In theory, all driverless cars will be equipped with V2V, and they will all abide by the same standardized protocols about the info that will be transmitted (there are ongoing discussions and deliberations on proposed protocols and approaches).

Whereas human drivers might variously choose to use a walkie-talkie or social media to let others know about the roadway status, presumably driverless cars will do so reliably and consistently. A human driver that might have been too lazy or not willing to aid their fellow mankind is going to be replaced by AI systems in driverless cars that will programmatically seek to transit what's happening on the streets.

That's great!

There you are, settled into a self-driving car on your way to work, and meanwhile, the AI of the self-driving car is engaging in a colossal electronic chitchat about the traffic situation, aiming to use that info to make your ride as efficient and effective as feasible.

There is a rub though.

Suppose you are on the freeway and your driverless car is surrounded by dozens upon dozens of other self-driving cars.

Keep in mind that there might be self-driving cars way up ahead of you.

There might be driverless cars some distance behind you.

There could be driverless cars right next to you.

If the freeway is elevated, there might be driverless cars below the freeway that are street driving.

More self-driving cars are sitting on the on-ramps leading into the freeway.

It's a vast herd of driverless cars, and all of them are vying for attention by transmitting the roadway status via V2V and trying to ascertain the roadway status by receiving and interpreting V2V messages from other self-driving cars.

Picture this as though you are standing in a crowded bar for a wild party and there are lots of discussions going on, the din is so loud and overwhelming that you can barely understand the person standing next to you as they try to carry on a conversation.

A cacophony of V2V messages might be less helpful than we all assume it will.

The AI that's driving the self-driving car that you are peacefully residing in might be getting a barrage of messages from those dozens upon dozens of other driverless cars.

Some of those messages are likely irrelevant to the existing driving task. For example, the V2V coming from the cars that are below the freeway is unlikely to be pertinent to the driving actions underway on the freeway.

Meanwhile, those driverless cars that are beneath the freeway are potentially keenly interested in the V2V coming from the cars on the freeway since perhaps they are intending to soon get onto the freeway and they are trying to find out what the traffic is like.

Consider other facets of when the V2V might not be especially helpful.

If a couch fell onto a lane, the first self-driving car to spot it would presumably send out a V2V to let other nearby driverless cars know that the couch is blocking the lane. Those nearby driverless cars then transmit the message to other further away self-driving cars, allowing those driverless cars a mile back or more to become aware of the couch issue. Think of the messaging as rippling like a wave.

How many such messages might be sent?

Well, without any predetermined means of coordination, each time that any of the driverless cars get the message they might opt to send it along to other self-driving cars, and simultaneously other driverless cars coming upon the debris will be sending out their own V2V messages saying the same thing (such messages shotgunning out in a fraction of second, each).

Zillions of messages all about the same instance are potentially now flying here and there (this is a mesh network, each car being a node, and communicating on a peer-to-peer basis, see the standard SAE 2735 for messaging details).

Suppose that a highway patrol car happened to be near the dropped couch and quickly pushed it out of the way.

Will nearby driverless cars transmit that the lane is no longer blocked?

Well, they might not do so since why send out that something is not blocked unless you realized that others might have prior awareness that it once was blocked. It could be that the self-driving cars just proceed now that the lane is no longer blocked and aren't necessarily going to update or rescind that the prior lane was blocked V2V messages.

Or, you might have all of them continuously transmitting whatever state of the driverless car is, once again emitting tons and tons of messages.

And so on.

It could be chaotic messaging, ending up as a sensory overload and being problematic for each AI system of each driverless car to figure out what's useful and what's not among the tsunami of messages.

Roadway Edge Computing

The overarching model of this use of V2V is one of no central coordination and instead a distributed form of V2V messaging.

One breakthrough approach being pursued involves using roadway edge computing as a concentrator and disseminator, putting small computers at key points along the roadway infrastructure that could aid in receiving the plethora of messages and trying to sort them out accordingly (for more on the rise of edge computing for this purpose, see **the link here**).

Such edge devices would then seek to reduce duplicative messaging, along with labeling and shunting along with messages in a compact and selective manner.

Though the driverless cars are still potentially deluging the airwaves with messages, the roadway edge computer is figuring out how to categorize and streamline the messages and then transmitting them smartly accordingly.

This would potentially cut down on the voluminous amount of V2V messages that any particular driverless car might have to closely examine. Using a filter, the AI might primarily look at the edge computer-generated messages and then selectively inspect V2V's coming from other driverless cars as warranted.

The V2V sensory overload to the AI of the driverless cars is potentially reduced.

One qualm is that there is a possible bottleneck due to the roadway edge computer, and if it is not quick enough or has a hiccup, the streamlined messaging will be undermined.

The counterargument is that the AI of the driverless cars would still be able to resort to examining the deluge of V2V's and would simply assume there is no edge device available, until or if the edge computer was able to continue proper operations.

Conclusion

Questions abound about the possibility of roadway edge computers:

- Who will pay for them to be put in place?

- Should this be done by the government or by private enterprises?

- How will the roadway edge computers be maintained?

- Will they be secure enough to avoid spoofing or cyber-hacking that could wreak havoc upon driverless cars that are relying upon those edge devices?

- Etc.

There's a classic line that it is hard to solve a problem for which the problem itself has not yet emerged.

In other words, we often aren't able to foresee new problems that will arise as a result of new innovations and technologies. As such, you aren't aware of and nor motivated to try and solve a problem that seemingly doesn't yet exist.

Dealing with the collaboration among self-driving cars is not yet a problem, and only once we have thousands of them, ultimately millions of driverless cars on our public roadways, are we apt to become concerned about these messaging difficulties.

Anyway, go ahead and put this one in your thinking cap and let's aim to solve a future problem before it becomes one.

CHAPTER 5

GROUND PENETRATING RADAR AND AI SELF-DRIVING CARS

CHAPTER 5
GROUND PENETRATING RADAR AND AI SELF-DRIVING CARS

Recent news reports have heralded the latest research on Ground Penetrating Radar (GPR) sensors and suggested that such devices will revolutionize the advent of AI-based self-driving cars.

Though it certainly will be exciting to potentially have GPR added into the mix of sensors used for achieving driverless cars, let's be cautious in overstating the possibilities.

I do not want to seem downbeat on GPR, and to be clear it is indeed a handy addition to self-driving car capabilities, but it won't radically change things and will take likely years to reach any viable and widespread adoption.

For those pursuing GPR, please keep going, full steam ahead.

Just know that the imagined gold that could be unearthed via producing and selling GPR for self-driving cars is not so easily grasped and some distance off in the future.

And, for those of you unfamiliar with GPR, don't be fooled by those that seem to imply that GPR will replace other sensory devices used on driverless cars.

Some of the media have gone so far as to suggest that GPR will replace cameras on driverless cars, which is a fundamental misunderstanding of what GPR does, plus a misunderstanding of how self-driving cars work.

The other facet to keep in mind is that even once GPR is better readied for real-world use in cars, it won't necessarily be tossed into all driverless cars, and instead potentially used on some brands and models, but not all.

That might seem to undercut to the market size potential, though there are going to be other uses of GPR and not solely designated for the advent of driverless cars (thus, GPR has other markets and opportunities to have strong growth).

Explaining GPR Capabilities

Here's what GPR does.

Using an electromagnetic sensory device, radar beams are broadcast downward from the surface into the subsurface. Based on reflections from the beams, the GPR tries to ascertain what might be underground, such as rocks, soil, roots, etc.

You might be puzzled as to why a self-driving car would care about the subsurface aspects (it's not as though an everyday passenger car has a digger or shovel that is seeking to dig up the road).

Essentially, the nature of the subsurface area detected is relatively unique and can be patterned into a signature or fingerprint.

If someone were to drive around and collect GPR data on existing roads, they could collect together the data and have a kind of descriptive signature of the roads, providing a map that's based on underground data.

Then, later on, any self-driving car that was unsure of what road it was on or where it might be on that roadway as to the location, could do a real-time snapshot of a GPR imprint as the driverless car was proceeding, and then compare the imprint to pre-mapped signatures, allowing it to reasonably conclude that whatever matches to the map is the likely position of the self-driving car.

It seems to some like a lot of work when you can just use a camera to "see" where you are or use a GPS or some other technique and refer to a conventional map.

Yes, the GPR is an "extraordinary" approach and not especially intended to replace those other methods of location identification, but it does come in handy in certain circumstances.

The most notable circumstance would be driving in snow.

While driving on a snowy road, sometimes the visual scene is obscured or otherwise confounded by the piling up of snow. You might also be in an area that doesn't have a strong GPS signal.

The handy dandy GPR might be your salvation in such a situation.

Despite not being able to see the road, there is still a chance of driving on the road, using the GPR to provide guidance to the AI driving controls.

We might all reasonably agree that driving based solely on the GPR would be dicey and not something of a preferable nature.

The odds are that the GPR would augment the other sensory devices and the data collected would be analyzed in concert with whatever else the other sensors are also indicating.

Okay, so GPR offers a predominantly augmented sensory capability and would find uses in somewhat narrow circumstances.

There is a bit of a rub.

If the underground signature or fingerprint hasn't already been mapped, the GPR won't really do you much good.

That's part of the odd twist.

Presumably, you would more than likely be using the GPR on rural roads, backroads, ones that are bound to have snow on them and for which snowplows are a rarity, but you then need to ponder whether anyone would have gone to the trouble to pre-map those roads so that they can be used for GPR in a driverless car.

A chicken and the egg conundrum.

There is obviously a cost and effort required to go around and do the GPR mappings.

Sure, maybe for some popular roads it would be worth the cost, while for less-traveled roads and ones off the beaten path, it would seem not quite as profitable to make such maps.

Thus, a self-driving car would have to be able to access above-ground maps, which are commonly available, and also underground maps, which don't exist today on any widespread basis and will need to be created.

Not wanting to crush the dreams of GPR, consider too that rain impacts the soil and cause difficulties in matching a real-time snapshot imprint with pre-recorded subsurface signatures.

Depending too on the type of roadway surface, there can be issues in penetrating downward, and the data collected might be noisy or partial in nature.

On the other hand, there are some interesting other potential uses.

For example, a multi-level parking garage could potentially be mapped for its roadway signatures (based not on soil but instead on the various concrete and steel elements that were used in the construction), and then a GPR used in a self-driving car could more readily navigate within the garage.

Yes, a nifty possibility.

Though, on a cost-benefit mindset, would the existing sensors be sufficient anyway, and would the added cost for the GPR outweigh this and its other potential use cases?

Time will tell.

Overall, the question arises: *To what degree will the advent of AI true self-driving cars be likely to add GPR into the mix of their sensor suites?*

Let's unpack the matter and see.

The Levels Of Self-Driving Cars

It is important to clarify what I mean when referring to AI-based true self-driving cars.

True self-driving cars are ones that the AI drives the car entirely on its own and there isn't any human assistance during the driving task.

These driverless vehicles are considered a Level 4 and Level 5, while a car that requires a human driver to co-share the driving effort is usually considered at a Level 2 or Level 3. The cars that co-share the driving task are described as being semi-autonomous, and typically contain a variety of automated add-on's that are referred to as ADAS (Advanced Driver-Assistance Systems).

There is not yet a true self-driving car at Level 5, which we don't yet even know if this will be possible to achieve, and nor how long it will take to get there.

Meanwhile, the Level 4 efforts are gradually trying to get some traction by undergoing very narrow and selective public roadway trials, though there is controversy over whether this testing should be allowed per se (we are all life-or-death guinea pigs in an experiment taking place on our highways and byways, some point out).

Since semi-autonomous cars require a human driver, the adoption of those types of cars won't be markedly different than driving conventional vehicles, so there's not much new per se to cover about them on this topic (though, as you'll see in a moment, the points next made are generally applicable).

For semi-autonomous cars, it is important that the public be forewarned about a disturbing aspect that's been arising lately, namely that in spite of those human drivers that keep posting videos of themselves falling asleep at the wheel of a Level 2 or Level 3 car, we all need to avoid being misled into believing that the driver can take away their attention from the driving task while driving a semi-autonomous car.

You are the responsible party for the driving actions of the vehicle, regardless of how much automation might be tossed into a Level 2 or Level 3.

Self-Driving Cars And GPR

GPR could be used in conventional cars and provide some form of visual display or audio indication to human drivers, serving as a secondary mapping system that offers guidance to drivers.

Perhaps some automakers will decide to include GPR into their Level 2 and Level 3 vehicles.

Besides providing a handy capability, the automakers choosing to use GPR would be able to tout that their cars are differentiated from those on the market that lack GPR.

It could be a substantive strategic advantage or feature that could entice drivers to buy those brands and models that have GPR.

If that did occur, the odds would seem that the other automakers might follow suit, in which case GPR would gradually become commonplace on most cars and become an assumed and everyday expected capability.

That would be a boon to GPR.

Once again, the added cost though for providing GPR would need to be ascertained and whether passing along those costs to those desirous of buying a car would "overprice" a car and hamper car sales.

In terms of true self-driving cars, since they rely entirely on sensory devices for detecting the driving environment, it would seem to some that it's a no-brainer to add GPR to any Level 4 and Level 5 driverless car.

The mantra oftentimes seems to be that the more the merrier when it comes to having various sensory types on a self-driving car.

Life isn't that easy.

The more sensory devices you add, the greater the cost of the vehicle.

Plus, think too about the ongoing maintenance and repairs associated with any sensory devices included in a driverless car.

You also need to consider the added weight to the car, and where you can even find a spot to place the sensory package.

Sensors on a driverless car cannot just be randomly placed into the body or structure of the car.

There are heat issues to be dealt with, along with routing electrical and communications cables to the device, etc.

Existing GPR devices are today rather large, bulky, and weighty.

Until the size comes down, and the weight, and the cost, and other such factors improve, it is pretty much a no-brainer to not include GPR, at least until it is readily viable for adoption on a widespread basis.

And, as emphasized, GPR won't be acting alone on a self-driving car.

This means that you need to integrate the GPR detection into the sensor fusion efforts, and figure out when, where, and how the GPR capability will square with the sensor efforts of the cameras, radar, LIDAR, ultrasonic, and whatever else is already loaded onto the car.

In fact, there is somewhat of a Darwinian process that might occur related to sensors on self-driving cars.

Rather than throwing the kitchen sink of all sensors onto a driverless car, it is likely that gradually the automakers and self-driving tech makers will begin to winnow down the set of sensors that are sufficient and complete to drive the vehicle.

You might say they are seeking a parsimonious set of sensors.

Or, more plainly, the Goldilocks set of sensors, not too many, not too few, and instead just the right amount.

Will GPR make that cut?

Time will tell.

Conclusion

GPR is not "new" per se.

Devices to scan what's underground have been around for years, used for exploring the subsurface on other planets and for earthly purposes of trying to detect landmines.

Cleverly, there has been a realization that GPR tech could be used for aiding driverless cars.

That is sensible and will generally be welcomed.

There are some hitches or hoops that need to be jumped through to get GPR ready for prime time use on self-driving cars and will take time to get ironed out.

One big question is whether the ship might sail before GPR is ready.

In other words, if the automakers and self-driving tech makers have proceeded along without GPR, and meshed together with their existing sensors into a coherent and rolled-out driverless car fleet, will they be willing to essentially retrofit their vehicles to accommodate GPR once it becomes viable?

Not sure.

Look into the future.

If self-driving cars are roaming around successfully, doing so without GPR (since it wasn't yet available for use when those driverless cars were first turned into production), why would an automaker go the trouble to add GPR?

It seems somewhat unlikely that you'd try to add it to the fleets already in existence, though of course such a retrofit would be possible at some likely exorbitant cost and logistics nightmare possibility.

The odds are that it would get added into the next-gen of self-driving cars instead.

Yet, there is still a cost to do so.

Besides the cost of the GPR device itself, there would be the cost of integrating the GPR into the vehicle and the cost of integrating the GPR into the systems that deal with sensor fusion.

Integrating an entirely new type of sensor into an existing system stack is not quite so easy.

Realize that the GPR would not be simply an isolated sensory component and would need to be integrated into the overarching sensor fusion activities.

This will force the system developers to deal with some thorny issues.

Well, for those developing GPR, do keep your nose to the grind and dig away at making GPR a viable choice for use on self-driving cars.

Gold might not necessarily be in them thar hills, but there's hopefully sufficient silver underground that will provide a handsome payoff.

CHAPTER 6

UPSTREAM PARABLE
AND
AI SELF-DRIVING CARS

CHAPTER 6

UPSTREAM PARABLE

AND

AI SELF-DRIVING CARS

It is parable time.

Some of you might be familiar with a parable that many refer to as the Upstream Parable or alternatively the River Story.

Attributed to various originating sources, some believe it was initially brought up in the 1930s by Saul Alinksy, political activist, and later by Irving Zola, medical sociologist, though it was perhaps given its greatest impetus via a paper by John McKinlay in 1975 that applied the parable to the domain of healthcare (and, where it has become a revered classic, repeatedly cited since then and used over and over in debates about healthcare systems).

I'll start with a slimmed-down version of the story.

You are walking along the bank of a rushing river when you spy a person in the water that seems to be drowning.

Heroically, you leap into the water and save the person.

So far, so good.

A few minutes later, another person floats by that seems to be drowning.

Once again, you jump into the river and save the person.

This keeps happening, again and again.

In each case, you dive in, and though you manage to save the person each such time, doing so denies you the chance to go upstream and ascertain why all these people are getting into the water to begin with, for which you might be able to bring the matter to an overall halt and prevent anyone else from further getting into the dangerous waters.

And that's the end of the story.

You might be thinking, what gives with this?

Why is it such a catchy parable?

By most interpretations, the story offers a metaphor about how we oftentimes are so busy trying to fix things that we don't pay attention to how they were originating.

Our efforts and focus go toward that which we immediately see.

And, especially when there is something demanding incessantly our rapt attention right away.

If you are able to take a breather and mull things over in such a situation, you might ultimately be able to solve the matter entirely by going upstream, make a fix there, rather than being battered over and over downstream.

In fact, it could be that one fix at the upstream would prevent all the rest of the downstream efforts, meaning that economically it is potentially a lot more sound to deal with the upstream rather than the frenetic and costly downstream activities.

This can be applied to healthcare in a myriad of ways.

For example, suppose that a populace has improper hygiene habits and lives in a manner that encourages disease to take hold.

Upon arriving at such a locale, your first thought might be to build a hospital to care for the sick.

After a while, the hospital maybe fills up, so you need to build another hospital.

On and on, this merry-go-round goes, devoting more and more resources to building hospitals to aid the ill.

It would be easy to fall into the mental trap of putting all your attention toward those hospitals.

You might chew-up your energy on dealing with:
- Are the hospitals running efficiently?
- Do hospitals have sufficient medical equipment?
- Can you keep enough nurses and doctors on-staff to handle the workloads?
- Etc.

Recalling the lesson of the Upstream Parable, maybe there ought to be attention given to how the populace is living and try to find ways to cut down on the breaking out of disease.

That's upstream and it is the point at which the production of ill people is taking place.

Imagine, if you did change the upstream to clean things up and prevent or at least reduce by a large measure the rampant disease, you'd no longer need such a large volume of hospitals, and nor all that equipment, and nor have the issues of staffing the medical teams in a large-scale way.

Notice too that everyone involved in the matter are doing what they believe best to do.

In other words, those building all those hospitals perceive a need to heal the sick, and so they are sincerely and genuinely "doing the right thing."

Unfortunately, they are consumed mightily by that task, akin to pulling drowning people out of the rushing river, and thus they fail to consider what's upstream and potentially better ways to "cure" the people of their ills.

Okay, that's the overarching gist of the upstream and downstream fable.

There are numerous variants of how the story is told.

Some like to say that the persons falling into the water are children and that you are therefore saving essentially helpless children (and, as though to go even further, sometimes the indication is that they are babies).

I guess that might make the parable more engaging, but it doesn't especially change the overall tenor of the lessons involved.

Here's one reason that some like to use children or babies in lieu of referring to adults.

A bizarrely distorted reaction by some is that if it is adults that are falling into the water, why aren't they astute enough to stop doing so, and why should it be that anyone else should be worried about saving adults that presumably should know better (thus, substituting children or babies makes that less arguable, but I must say that the somewhat cynical and bitter portrayal of adults is a bit alarming since it could be that something beyond their power is tossing them into the drink, and anyway it fights against the spirit of the parable overall).

Another variation of the story has a second individual that comes to aid in saving the drowning subjects.

At the end of the story, this second individual, after having helped to pull person after person out of the river, suddenly stops doing so and walks upstream.

The first individual, still steeped in pulling people out of the water, yells frantically to the second individual, imploring with grave concern, where are they going?

I'm going upstream to find out what's going on and aim to stop whoever is tossing people into the river, says the second individual.

End of story.

That's a nifty variant.

Why?

Well, in the first version, the person saving the lives has no chance to do anything but continue to save lives (we can reasonably conclude that if the saving were to be curtailed, person after person would drown).

In the second version, we hope or assume that the first individual can sufficiently continue to save lives, while the second person scoots upstream to try and do something about the predicament.

Of course, life is never that clear cut.

It could be that the second person leaving will lamentedly present a serious and life-denying result at the downstream saving-lives position.

In which case, we need to ponder as to whether it is better to keep saving lives in the immediate, rather than trying to solve the problem overall, or that you must make a death sentence decision to essentially abandon some to their deaths in order to deal with the problem by sorting out its root.

On a related topic, nearly all seasoned software developers and AI builders tend to know that whenever you have a budding system that is exhibiting problems, you seek to find the so-called root cause.

If you spend all your time trying to fix errors being generated by the root cause, you'll perpetually be in a bind of just fixing those errors and never stop the flow.

Anyway, the variant to the parable is quite handy since it brings up a devilish dilemma.

While in the midst of dealing with a crisis, can you spare time and effort toward the root cause, or would that meanwhile generate such adverse consequences that you are risking greater injury by not coping with the immediate and direct issues at-hand?

Keep in mind too that just because the second person opts to walk upstream, we have no way of knowing whether the upstream exploration will even be successful.

It could be that the upstream problem is so distant that the second individual never gets there, and in which case, if meanwhile, people were drowning, it was quite a hefty price to pay for having not solved the root problem.

Or, maybe the second individual finds the root, but they are unable to fix it quickly (maybe it's a troll that is too large to battle, and instead the second individual has to try and prevent people from wandering into its trap, but this only cuts down on say one-third of the pace of people getting tossed into the river).

This means that for some period of time, those drowning are going to keep drowning.

Here's an even sadder possibility.

The second individual reaches the upstream root and tries to fix the problem, yet somehow, regrettably, makes it worse (maybe it was a bridge that people were falling off, and while attempting to fix the bridge, the second individual messed-up and the bridge is even more precarious than it was before!).

It could be that up until then, the first individual was able to keep up with saving those drowning, and now, ironically, after the second individual tried to fix the problem, and in the meantime wasn't around to help save the drowning victims, there are a slew more people falling into the water, completely overwhelming the first individual.

Yikes!

As you can see, I like this latter version that includes the second individual, allowing us to extend the lessons that can be readily gleaned from the parable.

Some though prefer using the simpler version.

It all depends upon the point that you are trying to drive home by using the tale.

For those of you that are smarmy, I'm sure that you've already come up with other variations.

Why not make a net that is stretched across the river and catches all those people?

There, problem solved, you proudly proclaim.

Well, which problem?

The problem of the people drowning at the downstream position, or the problem of the people being tossed into the river and possibly leading to being drowned (hopefully, they don't drown *before* they reach your net).

In any case, yes, it might be sensible to come up with a more effective or efficient way to save the drowning persons.

That doesn't though necessarily negate the premise that it is the root that deserves attention, but I appreciate that you've tried to find a means to reduce the effort at the downstream, which maybe frees up those that are aiming to go upstream to find and fix the root cause.

Bravo.

One other last facet to mention, and it somewhat dovetails into the notion of creating and putting in place the net, sometimes there is such a massive setup of infrastructure at the downstream that it becomes unwieldy and takes on a life of its own to deal with.

Furthermore, and the twist upon a twist, suppose that the net gets nearly all, but a few happen to go underwater and aren't saved by the net.

Imagine someone standing downstream of the (already) downstream net.

They might end up in the same parable, and upon coming up to find you and your net, believe they have found the root cause.

It could be that the root cause is further upstream and that there are lots of other intervening downstream solutions, all of which are (hopefully) mitigating the upstream, yet it might be difficult to figure out what's the root versus what's not the root.

There could be a nearly infinite series of downstream solutions, all well-meaning, each of which makes the whole affair incredibly complex and confounding, while there might be an elegant end to the monstrosity by somehow getting to the real root.

Well, that was quite an instructive look at the fable.

You might be wondering, can the fable be used in other contexts, such as something AI-related (that's why I'm here).

Yes, indeed, here's an interesting question to ponder: *"Will the advent of AI-based true self-driving cars potentially find itself getting mired in downstream matters akin to the Upstream Parable?"*

Let's unpack the matter and see.

The Levels Of Self-Driving Cars

It is important to clarify what I mean when referring to AI-based true self-driving cars.

True self-driving cars are ones that the AI drives the car entirely on its own and there isn't any human assistance during the driving task.

These driverless vehicles are considered a Level 4 and Level 5, while a car that requires a human driver to co-share the driving effort is usually considered at a Level 2 or Level 3. The cars that co-share the driving task are described as being semi-autonomous, and typically contain a variety of automated add-on's that are referred to as ADAS (Advanced Driver-Assistance Systems).

There is not yet a true self-driving car at Level 5, which we don't yet even know if this will be possible to achieve, and nor how long it will take to get there.

Meanwhile, the Level 4 efforts are gradually trying to get some traction by undergoing very narrow and selective public roadway trials, though there is controversy over whether this testing should be allowed per se (we are all life-or-death guinea pigs in an experiment taking place on our highways and byways, some point out).

Since semi-autonomous cars require a human driver, the adoption of those types of cars won't be markedly different than driving conventional vehicles, so there's not much new per se to cover about them on this topic (though, as you'll see in a moment, the points next made are generally applicable).

For semi-autonomous cars, it is important that the public be forewarned about a disturbing aspect that's been arising lately, namely that in spite of those human drivers that keep posting videos of themselves falling asleep at the wheel of a Level 2 or Level 3 car, we all need to avoid being misled into believing that the driver can take away their attention from the driving task while driving a semi-autonomous car.

You are the responsible party for the driving actions of the vehicle, regardless of how much automation might be tossed into a Level 2 or Level 3.

Self-Driving Cars And The Parable

For Level 4 and Level 5 true self-driving vehicles, there won't be a human driver involved in the driving task.

All occupants will be passengers.

The AI is doing the driving.

Sounds pretty good.

No need for any arcane fables or tall tales.

But, wait, give the Upstream Parable a chance.

Some today are arguing that more regulation is needed at the federal level to provide guidance over how self-driving cars will be designed, built, and fielded.

In fact, those proponents tend to say that having the states or local authorities in cities and counties having to come up with guidelines for the use of self-driving cars is counterproductive.

You might be surprised to know that many of the automakers and self-driving tech firms seem to generally agree with the notion that the guidelines ought to be at the federal level.

Why?

One reason would be the presumed simplicity of having an across-the-board set of rules, rather than having to adjust or craft the AI system and driverless car to accommodate a potential morass of thousands upon thousands of varying rules across the entire country.

On the other hand, a cogent argument is made that having a singular federal level approach might not allow for sufficient flexibility and tailoring that befits the needs of local municipalities.

Let's suppose that the local approach prevails (I'm not making such a proclamation, it's just a what-if).

If self-driving cars have trouble coping at the local levels, we might become focused on the downstream matters.

Meanwhile, one might contend that it was the upstream that needed to provide an overarching approach that was sufficient to abate the downstream issues.

There's a lot more to this debate and I don't want to oversimplify it, but we need to move on because I have other fish to fry herein.

Back to the parable we go.

Suppose a fleet of self-driving cars is owned by a particular automaker.

The self-driving cars communicate with a cloud-based system, via OTA (Over-The-Air) electronic capabilities, and pull down patches and updates to the AI system that's on-board, and also the on-board system uploads collected sensory data and other info from the self-driving car.

Pretend that something goes awry in the self-driving cars of that fleet.

Do you try to quickly deal with each individual self-driving car, which might be on the roadway and endangering passengers, pedestrians, or other human-driven cars, or do you try to ferret out the root cause and then see if you can get that patch shoved out to the fleet in-time?

Some assert that this very kind of issue is why there ought to be a kill button or kill switch inside all self-driving cars, allowing presumably for a human passenger to make a decision right there in the driverless car to stop it from processing.

I've elucidated that this isn't as robust an approach as most seem to assume.

In any case, you could liken this to the upstream versus downstream fable.

Pleasingly, once again, lessons revealed due to a handy underlying schema or template.

Conclusion

Generally, the Upstream Parable is pretty handy for lots of circumstances.

Part of the reason it is so memorable is due to the aspect that it captures innately what we see each and every day, and helps to bring to light the otherwise hidden or unrealized elements of systems around us that we are immersed in.

While standing at the DMV and waiting endlessly to get your driver's license renewed, you have to let your mind wander to keep your sanity and wonder whether you've found yourself floating in the downstream waters.

Drowning in paperwork!

If the DMV had its act together, there'd be a solution at the root that would make your desire to renew your driver's license a bit less arduous and frustrating.

For sanity sake, go ahead and use the fable to your heart's content and keep finding ways to balance the downstream with the upstream, aiming to prevent problems before they arise and make the world a better place.

That's a good lesson no matter how you cut it.

CHAPTER 7
RED-LIGHT AUTO-STOPPING AND AI SELF-DRIVING CARS

CHAPTER 7

RED-LIGHT AUTO-STOPPING

AND

AI SELF-DRIVING CARS

Human drivers seem to effortlessly be able to detect red lights of traffic signals.

Well, most of the time.

Sometimes, a driver is distracted and fails to spot the red light, blowing right through it.

It could be that a driver isn't necessarily distracted, and might instead simply be in an unfamiliar locale, and fails to spy where the traffic signal has been placed.

Another possibility is that the red light is somehow obscured, perhaps there's heavy rain coming down or snow that's falling, any of which might make things harder for the driver to see a traffic signal.

Scarily, there are those drivers that are intoxicated and thus they might or might not detect a red-light, and even if they do see it, their mental state might disrupt them from taking the proper action and coming to a stop.

Some drivers like to play a game of chicken with red lights, whereby upon seeing a red light up ahead, the driver keeps in-motion, though they should really be slowing down, but they believe in their own minds that they can comfortably end-up at the light once it turns green and won't need to come to a stop (this is a daily judgment call, by many).

In some cases, they judge wrong, and end-up either partially into the intersection or decide to just go for it and drive through the red light entirely.

Then there are the outright scofflaws.

These drivers don't care that the light is red.

They are willing to rush through a red light as though it were a green light.

Why?

One popular excuse is that there wasn't any other cross-traffic (that they could see), and thus why come to a stop, they exhort, and anyway it wastes energy to come to a stop and then get underway again (those that are so-called crying tears over such wasted energy are unlikely to be prolonged savers of energy in any other respects of their existence, by the way).

You can potentially add to the list of intentions for not stopping knowingly at a red light the aspect of the driver believing fervently that they won't get caught.

In other words, it's one thing to run a red light, breaking the law, and get caught doing so, while there's the other side of things when you are pretty sure that you won't be caught doing this illegal act.

Sadly, some people are guided by their chances or probability of being caught driving badly, more so than whether their driving actions generate ill-advised risks that could demonstrably harm or kill themselves or others (including their passengers, nearby pedestrians, and drivers and passengers in other cars).

Yes, our daily driving in our local neighborhoods and downtown areas are rife with an ongoing dance of the red-light ballet.

You might be the safest driver out there, and yet you know that at any time, at any place there's a traffic signal, other drivers might be misjudging or purposely flouting a red light, and could readily smash into your car.

There's not too much you can do, other than be watching endlessly for the actions of other drivers and hope that you'll be lucky enough and quick enough to spot a red-light hoodlum and avoid their adverse driving antics.

Fortunately, there isn't as much red-light deadly outcomes per year than you might otherwise assume.

Let's though temper that point with this sobering statistic, an estimated 1,000 people per year in the United States are killed by a red-light driving incident.

That's about 2 to 3 people per day, on average, so think of this as a loved one or someone that you know, any of which could be caught up in a red-light fatality.

I am loathed to say it, but the odds of getting killed via a red-light thug is relatively low (my hesitation is that I don't want those idiots that are running red lights to somehow interpret the stat as though somehow it is okay for them to do their terrifying and dastardly acts of red-light destruction).

In the United States alone, we drive nearly 3.2 trillion miles per year.

There are approximately 300,000 traffic signals that we can encounter during our driving travels throughout the country.

All in all, for the number of miles that we collectively drive, and for the number of traffic signals that you might encounter on a daily driving trip, there aren't as many red-light running wipeouts as could occur.

Once again, be careful in interpreting that aspect.

I'm betting that we all see or experience a red-light dangerous act with a rather common frequency.

By luck of the draw or maybe due to other circumstances, those red-light crazies aren't being continually turned into killer roadway incidents.

Yet, they are happening, nonetheless.

According to a survey of American drivers, reportedly one-third or about 30% or so have stated that they blew through a red light in the last 30 days.

Yikes!

In fact, apparently, about 40% of all drivers were also of the belief that if they did run a red-light, they figured it was unlikely they would get caught.

That last statistic makes sense since the odds of getting caught running a red light involves the chances of a police car being at the same intersection at the same moment that you run the red light, along with the cop realizing that you've done so, which can be tricky to readily spot at times.

If you ever wondered why some cities decide to use red-light cameras to try and catch the red-light evildoers, perhaps the aspect that nearly a half of all drivers believe they won't get caught showcases that if someone realizes a camera might catch them, it would deter those malcontents that are contemplating such an action (though realize that many oftentimes don't even notice the camera anyway, and thus, it becomes an after-the-fact lesson rather than a preventative cure per se).

Estimates are that over the course of a year, you might end-up sitting at red-lights for about 60 hours of your lifetime annually (that's adding up all the times in a year that you stop at a red light).

The typical traffic signal has about a two-minute or so cycle time, meaning that it goes through the cycle of green, yellow, and red in about a two minute time period (this varies quite a bit in terms of some locations might have cycles of 90 seconds, or maybe three minutes, four minutes, etc.).

A rule-of-thumb is that the yellow light is usually around 3 to 6 seconds in length (again, this varies)

Thus, in theory, the green light and red light split the rest of the two minutes or so cycle time.

Sometimes, the green light gets the greater proportion, while in certain intersections or particular times of the day, the red light gets the larger proportion of the cycle time.

Why all this discussion about the nature of red lights?

The latest news reports claim that Tesla is readying an AutoPilot update that will include a red-light auto-stopping feature.

Sparking the excitement was a video posted that purportedly shows the red-light feature in use while a driver was driving his Tesla (here's the link).

On the one hand, it would certainly seem like a great advantage to have a car that automatically comes to a stop when there's a red-light.

In theory, it would do away with the litany of red-light qualms and human foibles that I've just meticulously walked you through.

Hurrah!

But real-life is not always so easily swayed or overcome.

There are a lot of gotchas and this coming update, if indeed it is on the verge of being released, could be a bad deal.

There are lots of ways that this can go wrong, horrifically so.

Not only could this harm people, but it also has the potential for creating a backlash against Tesla cars and could potentially have a backlash overspill toward all efforts underway to craft and field true AI-based self-driving cars.

Here's today's question: *"Will the advent of a Tesla AutoPilot update that includes a red-light auto-stopping feature have potentially adverse consequences and what might those be precipitated by?"*

Let's unpack the matter and see.

The Levels Of Self-Driving Cars

It is important to clarify what I mean when referring to AI-based true self-driving cars.

True self-driving cars are ones that the AI drives the car entirely on its own and there isn't any human assistance during the driving task.

These driverless vehicles are considered a Level 4 and Level 5, while a car that requires a human driver to co-share the driving effort is usually considered at a Level 2 or Level 3.

The cars that co-share the driving task are described as being semi-autonomous, and typically contain a variety of automated add-on's that are referred to as ADAS (Advanced Driver-Assistance Systems).

There is not yet a true self-driving car at Level 5, which we don't yet even know if this will be possible to achieve, and nor how long it will take to get there.

Meanwhile, the Level 4 efforts are gradually trying to get some traction by undergoing very narrow and selective public roadway trials, though there is controversy over whether this testing should be allowed per se (we are all life-or-death guinea pigs in an experiment taking place on our highways and byways, some point out).

Since semi-autonomous cars require a human driver, the adoption of those types of cars won't be markedly different than driving conventional vehicles, so there's not much new per se to cover about them on this topic (though, as you'll see in a moment, the points next made are generally applicable).

For semi-autonomous cars, it is important that the public is forewarned about a disturbing aspect that's been arising lately, namely that in spite of those human drivers that keep posting videos of themselves falling asleep at the wheel of a Level 2 or Level 3 car, we all need to avoid being misled into believing that the driver can take away their attention from the driving task while driving a semi-autonomous car.

You are the responsible party for the driving actions of the vehicle, regardless of how much automation might be tossed into a Level 2 or Level 3.

Self-Driving Cars And Auto-Stopping

For Level 4 and Level 5 true self-driving vehicles, there won't be a human driver involved in the driving task.

All occupants will be passengers.

The AI is doing the driving.

Existing Tesla's are not Level 4 and nor are they Level 5.

Most would classify them as Level 2 today.

What difference does that make?

Well, if you have a true self-driving car (Level 4 and Level 5), one that is being driven solely by the AI, there is no need for a human driver and indeed no interaction between the AI and a human driver.

For a Level 2 car, the human driver is still in the driver's seat.

Furthermore, the human driver is considered the responsible party for driving that car.

The twist that's going to mess everyone up is that the AI might seem to be able to drive the Level 2 car, meanwhile, it cannot, and thus the human driver still must be attentive and act as though they are driving the car.

Consider how this applies to red lights.

You are driving a car and there is a red light up ahead.

The smiley face version of such a scenario is that the car detects the red light, and furthermore, upon the detection, brings the car to a stop, sufficiently in time to come to a stop smoothly and properly.

The human driver didn't have to take any action.

Score one point.

Imagine though that the car fails to detect the red light.

Presumably, the human driver is paying rapt attention and will realize that the red-light detection has gone awry, for whatever reason, and thus the human driver has to now bring the car to a stop for the red-light.

Will though human drivers have this required rapt attention.

If you relied upon the red-light auto-stopping feature and it successfully worked say ten times in a row, what impulse or reaction might you have as a human driver on subsequent red lights?

Of course, you'd begin to assume that the red-light auto-stopper will always save your bacon.

That's just human nature.

The drivers of cars with a red-light auto-stopper are going to be lulled into complacency.

You can bet that they'll believe so resolutely in the auto-stopper that they will readily take their eyes off the road and their hands off the wheel and their feet off the pedals.

Maybe this will be sufficient for say 90% of the time, or for those that are staunch believers, let's say it is even 99% of the time – you have to ask, what about the 10% or the 1% of the time that the auto-stopper didn't work right.

Time to score a minus point, likely make it several minus points.

I'm sure some will retort that there's no reason to believe that the auto-stopper won't work all of the time.

Really?

Suppose the red-light itself is obscured in some manner and not readily detected by the car?

Or, there is a red-light, but the system of the car fails to realize that it is the red-light of a traffic signal.

Keep in mind that when driving on a busy road that is in a downtown area, there are a lot of other competing red lights that have nothing to do with the traffic signals.

You are betting that the detection system is infallible.

Not a wise bet.

You might wonder, well, if that's the case, why would a fully true self-driving car be any better, since it would presumably have the same chances of fouling up (and, for a Level 2 car, at least the human driver is there as a means to step-in)?

First, this is exactly why the progress toward achieving public roadway ready Level 4 and Level 5 self-driving cars is slow going and a slugfest (by-and-large, there is a human safety driver sitting in the driver's seat currently, purposely monitoring the car and presumably ready to take over, and in theory alert at all times, unlike a conventional human driver).

The true self-driving car needs to be right, all of the time.

That's a high bar.

Secondly, many are anticipating that for true self-driving cars, they will be driving in designated areas, called an Operational Design Domain (ODD), which basically means the scope of where the self-driving car is able to drive.

Thus, you might have a Level 4 self-driving car that is set up to drive in a downtown area, during daylight, and not in inclement weather.

If those conditions aren't met, the self-driving car won't try driving, since it would be doing so outside of its allowed bounds.

In addition, many of the self-driving car developers are aiming to have detailed pre-mapped indications of where all the traffic signals are in the designated locale, which increases the chances of the system detecting the traffic signal and reduces the risk of mistaking something else as a traffic signal.

Some are also betting on the eventuality of V2I (vehicle-to-infrastructure) electronic communication.

This means that the roadway infrastructure such as traffic signals, bridges, railroad crossings, and other aspects will be equipped with an electronic device allowing those roadway elements to broadcast their status. Self-driving cars will be similarly equipped with V2I features to pick up the signals and therefore use that information accordingly.

Thus, in the future, a traffic signal will likely emit an electronic signal saying it is red, or green, or yellow, and the self-driving car won't necessarily need to visually spy the traffic signal (or, do so in conjunction with a visual double-check).

All of that is going to bolster the advent of self-driving cars.

That's not where things are today.

A Level 2 car that gets equipped with a red-light auto-stopping feature is asking for troubles.

And, in case you doubt that assertion, here's something you can bet your bottom dollar on.

When an incident happens of a Level 2 car that fails to stop for a red-light, and someone gets harmed or killed, the maker of the Level 2 car is going to say that it was unfortunate, but that in-the-end, the human driver was at fault.

Some really vigorous fans of a Level 2 car might say, hey, if a driver of a Level 2 wants to take a chance and use the red-light auto-stopper, and they get killed, it's on them.

Recall that a red-light incident isn't going to only endanger the driver of the car, it also endangers the passengers, and pedestrians nearby, and other drivers and their passengers.

Of the red-light deadly incidents taking place in our everyday conventional cars, about one-third or around 30% of those killed consisted of the driver of the offending car, while two-thirds were others that got entrapped into the matter.

Conclusion

There are some other facets to consider.

Suppose a Level 2 car with a red-light auto-stopper detects a red-light that isn't a traffic signal and inadvertently classifies the red-light as though it were associated with a traffic signal.

What would the auto-stopper do?

Presumably, it will do its thing, namely, it will try to bring the car to a stop.

If this happens, and say there's another car behind the stopping vehicle, the other driver (presumably a human) might get caught off-guard and ram into the Level 2 car that is unexpectedly coming to a halt.

Would the human driver of the car with the auto-stopper realize that the system has falsely opted to come to a stop, and if so, would the human driver be astute enough to timely overtake the action?

The bottom line is whether human drivers can really co-share the driving task with a red-light auto-stopper, such that the human driver will always be on their toes and able to course correct for the auto-stopper.

Plus, any such course correction has to be done on a timely basis, giving the human driver perhaps just a few seconds or a split second to decide what to do.

And, if the auto-stopper hasn't done its thing, the human driver might be overly concentrating on why the auto-stopper didn't act, rather than trying to resolve the red-light situation at hand.

Finally, in addition to the human lives question, some pundits suggest that if a Level 2 car does end-up involving human harm via an auto-stopper feature, the public and regulators might not comprehend why things went afoul, and instead try to put the kibosh on all efforts to craft and adopt self-driving cars altogether.

Accordingly, some that are worried about these potential adverse outcomes and argue that a red-light ought to be shined toward stopping the rollout of such a red-light auto-stopping feature.

Time will tell.

CHAPTER 8

FALSENESS OF SUPERHUMAN AI SELF-DRIVING CARS

CHAPTER 8

FALSENESS OF SUPERHUMAN
AI SELF-DRIVING CARS

Superhuman.

What does that mean?

What does that mean to you?

Well, Elon Musk has suggested that Tesla cars outfitted with self-driving tech "can definitely be superhuman" (in his tweet on April 7, 2020), which invokes the superhuman moniker and raises questions about what exactly the notion of being "superhuman" portends.

Regrettably, he is joined by a slew of others, both outside the field of AI and even many within the AI field, continuing to proudly and with apparent abandon banty around the superhuman signature.

The problem is that "superhuman" is a lousy form of terminology, allowing for inflated allusions to what AI is today, and merely is excessive over-the-top hype and an outright misnomer that spreads marketing blarney more so than offering bona fide substance.

Some might say that those with a bitter distaste for the use of "superhuman" might be overly tightly wound and should just loosen up about the matter.

No big deal, it would seem.

The counterargument is that in light of the heaps upon heaps of hyperbole going on about AI, there has to be somebody, someplace, and at some point-in-time with a willingness and verve that will start drawing a line in the sand, as it were.

One such line would be at the shameless and mindless invoking of the superhuman imagery.

Why pick on superhuman as the straw that breaks the camel's back?

Because it has a visceral stickiness that is going to keep it in use and likely get worse and worse in expanding usage over time.

In short, it sounds nice and catches the imagination, and akin to a veritable snowball, it just keeps rolling ahead, becoming bigger and bigger in popularity as it lumbers down the AI hysteria mountain.

Other ways of hyping AI are often more scientific-sounding and less catchy for the general public.

The "super" part in superhuman dovetails into our fascination and beloved adulation of the vaunted superman and superwomen comic books, movies, merchandising, etc., and now has become a kind of general lore in our contemporary society (the character of Superman was first showcased on April 18, 1938, in Action Comics #1).

Let's tackle what superhuman even seems to mean.

Suppose someone creates a checkers playing computer program, using AI, and it is able to beat all comers of a human variety.

In 1994, human player Marion Tinsley, a checkers world champion, fell to a checkers playing program called Chinook in a closely watched and highly publicized match, a moment that some assert was the point at which checkers exceeded humans at the game of checkers.

It has been said that AI checkers playing games have become superhuman.

Really?

Are we really willing to ascribe the notion of being superhuman due to the aspect that a computer program was able to best a top-ranked human checkers player?

By the way, many of the games played were draws.

Does that change your opinion about the superhuman capability of the checkers program?

If it was so superhuman, why didn't it whip the human in each and every game played, knocking the human player for a loop and showcasing how really super it is.

Anyway, the key point is that flinging around the superhuman catchphrase can be done by anyone and for whatever reason, they might arbitrarily choose.

You see, there isn't a formal definition per se of superhuman.

At least not a definition that all have agreed upon and furthermore, nor agreed to reserve for use in only proper settings (kind of like a "Break Glass" when superhuman is warranted or needed).

This brings up another facet.

Checkers is an interesting game, but it certainly isn't the most challenging of games (oops, sorry to you checkers fans, please don't go berserk; it's a great game, but you have to admit it is not as complex as say Go, Chess, and the like).

Does being "superhuman" count when the underlying task itself is not the topmost of challenges per se?

Suppose an AI system is able to cook a souffle and the resulting delicacy receives raves as the best ever by anyone, human hands included.

Superhuman!

Superhuman?

Okay, you might say, let's make the stakes higher and use something that humanity has mentally strained to do well for eons, such as the playing of chess.

Chess is a tough game.

We marvel at those human players that can play chess in ways that are a beauty to behold.

In 1997, an IBM chess playing game running on the Deep Blue supercomputer was able to win against human chess champion Garry Kasparov.

Was that program something we can rightfully refer to as superhuman?

Chess is something that most humans don't do well, and thus it would seem that the program was pretty impressive, along with beating our considered best at the game.

Keep in mind that the only thing the program could do is play chess.

It couldn't write a song, it couldn't carry on a Socratic open-ended dialogue with you, and otherwise used various programming "tricks" such as having in computer memory tons and tons of prior chess positions that it could rapidly search and make use of.

This doesn't seem to be especially super, nor superhuman.

Don't misunderstand and misinterpret such a "condemnation" – this does not imply that those superb chess-playing programs and checkers playing programs aren't tremendous accomplishments.

They are!

And, for each instance whereby via the use of AI techniques that we make further progress toward achieving (eventually) true AI, it's something worthy of applauding and offering some kind of trophy or recognition for those triumphs.

But, using a medal or crown that implies being capable of human efforts, and indeed implies the ability to go beyond human efforts, presumably far beyond human efforts as a result of being "super," that's not an appropriate way to offer praise.

Consider too the role of common-sense reasoning.

Humans have common-sense reasoning.

As an aside, I realize some might chuckle and say that they know some people that lack in common-sense, but, putting aside such snickering, there is something called common-sense that humans do undeniably seem to have overall (see my analysis of common-sense reasoning at **this link here**).

There isn't any AI system today that has anything close to what human common-sense reasoning seems to entail.

So, if an AI system is "superhuman," does it count that the AI doesn't have a core aspect of human capability, namely that the AI lacks common-sense reasoning?

Wouldn't you tend to assume that something of a superhuman caliber ought to be able to do everything that a human can do, and on top of that, go beyond human reach and be super?

That just seems logical.

Again, it might appear that this is blowing out of proportion the use of "superhuman" as a means to describe AI systems, yet do realize that many aren't aware of the true limitations and narrowness involved in these AI systems that some are saying are superhuman.

The subtle attachment of "superhuman" to an AI system provides a glow of incredible essence, and inch by inch is convincing the public that AI can do wonderous things of a superhuman nature, all of which creates outsized expectations and sets people up to be misled and less wary of what AI is able to actually do today.

Take another consideration, brittleness.

Many of the Machine Learning (ML) and Deep Learning (DL) systems that are being deployed today are brittle at the edges of what they do.

A facial recognition system that is developed by using ML/DL could be really good at detecting people by their faces, and yet it also can fail to do so when a face is partially obscured or in other circumstances, which, by the way, other humans might not falter at.

Does that facial recognition deserve the superhuman label?

You might say that it does because in some respects it exceeds human ability to recognize faces, but at the same time, this hides the fact that facial recognition is actually worse than human capability in many ways.

Plus, as mentioned about common-sense reasoning, the AI facial recognition has no "there" in terms of understanding that the face so recognized is a human being and what a human being is or does. For the AI system, the face is a mathematical construct, no more significant than counting beans.

If something is superhuman, it seems like it ought to be super in all respects, and not brittle or weak in ways that undermine the "super" part of what it is getting as accolades.

With all of that as background, now let's turn our attention to true self-driving cars.

Here's the question for today: *Do AI-based true self-driving cars deserve to get the superhuman tribute, and if so, when or how will we know that it is appropriate and fair to do so?*

That's a great question.

Let's unpack the matter and see.

The Levels Of Self-Driving Cars

It is important to clarify what I mean when referring to AI-based true self-driving cars.

True self-driving cars are ones that the AI drives the car entirely on its own and there isn't any human assistance during the driving task.

These driverless vehicles are considered a Level 4 and Level 5, while a car that requires a human driver to co-share the driving effort is usually considered at a Level 2 or Level 3. The cars that co-share the driving task are described as being semi-autonomous, and typically contain a variety of automated add-on's that are referred to as ADAS (Advanced Driver-Assistance Systems).

There is not yet a true self-driving car at Level 5, which we don't yet even know if this will be possible to achieve, and nor how long it will take to get there.

Meanwhile, the Level 4 efforts are gradually trying to get some traction by undergoing very narrow and selective public roadway trials, though there is controversy over whether this testing should be allowed per se (we are all life-or-death guinea pigs in an experiment taking place on our highways and byways, some point out).

Since semi-autonomous cars require a human driver, the adoption of those types of cars won't be markedly different than driving conventional vehicles, so there's not much new per se to cover about them on this topic (though, as you'll see in a moment, the points next made are generally applicable).

For semi-autonomous cars, it is important that the public needs to be forewarned about a disturbing aspect that's been arising lately, namely that in spite of those human drivers that keep posting videos of themselves falling asleep at the wheel of a Level 2 or Level 3 car, we all need to avoid being misled into believing that the driver can take away their attention from the driving task while driving a semi-autonomous car.

You are the responsible party for the driving actions of the vehicle, regardless of how much automation might be tossed into a Level 2 or Level 3.

Self-Driving Cars And Pondering Superhuman

For Level 4 and Level 5 true self-driving vehicles, there won't be a human driver involved in the driving task.

All occupants will be passengers.

The AI is doing the driving.

Existing Tesla's are not Level 4 and nor are they Level 5.

Most would classify them as Level 2 today.

What difference does that make?

Well, if you have a true self-driving car (Level 4 and Level 5), one that is being driven solely by the AI, there is no need for a human driver and indeed no interaction between the AI and a human driver.

For a Level 2 car, the human driver is still in the driver's seat.

Furthermore, the human driver is considered the responsible party for driving that car.

The twist that's going to mess everyone up is that the AI might seem to be able to drive the Level 2 car, meanwhile, it cannot, and thus the human driver still must be attentive and act as though they are driving the car.

With that as a crucial backdrop, here's the tweet that Elon Musk sent on April 7, 2020: "Humans drive using 2 cameras on a slow gimbal & are often distracted. A Tesla with 8 cameras, radar, sonar & always being alert can definitely be superhuman."

The first part of his tweet makes a physics-clever reference to human eyes, saying that they are like two cameras, and our two eyes and head are mounted on our necks, akin to a slow gimbal that allows us to look back-and-forth while driving a car.

In terms of human drivers succumbing to being distracted while driving, this indeed is a serious and quite troubling problem, along with drivers being intoxicated and otherwise succumbing to a host of human foibles while at the wheel of a car.

Sadly, in the United States alone, there are about 40,000 deaths each year due to car crashes, and an estimated 2.5 million injuries annually.

The hope is that true self-driving cars will avoid incurring as many of those deaths and injuries as possible.

Some believe that we are going to have zero deaths, but this doesn't make logical sense since there will still be some deaths involved in car crashes, regardless if we somehow magically even had only self-driving cars on our roadways (for why zero deaths is a zero chance).

Suppose that true self-driving cars are able to reduce the number of car-related deaths and injuries, does that constitute that the AI and the self-driving car are superhuman?

It is tempting to perhaps give the AI such a prize, especially since the task at hand involves life-or-death.

A checkers or chess-playing AI system is obviously not involved in life-or-death circumstances (unless, perhaps, there's a dual-to-the-death on the line as part of the match, something we don't do anymore).

In short, the AI for a self-driving car has a lot going for it in terms of possibly being a candidate to get the honor of being considered superhuman.

It involves the complexities of driving a car, it entails life-or-death matters, and if it can presumably drive more reliably than humans then it seems to be able to drive better than humans do.

Still, does that attain a superhuman quality?

Essentially, the AI is driving as well as humans, minus the foibles of humans.

The impression one might get from calling it superhuman is that the AI can get the car out of dire situations, magically causing the car to avoid going off a cliff or somehow cause the car to suddenly sprout wings and fly out of danger.

That's not what a Level 4 or Level 5 self-driving is going to do.

You could give it the "more-reliable-human" phraseology (if there was such a thing), but superhuman seems excessive.

Now, all of that discussion covers generically the advent of true self-driving cars.

Elon was referring to specifically the Tesla cars, including their cameras, radar, and sonar.

For those of you in-the-know, you probably noticed that he didn't mention LIDAR (an additional type of sensor device, being used by just about everyone in self-driving cars other than Tesla), a sore topic, and one that still is an open question as to whether it is feasible to achieve true self-driving cars without LIDAR (Elon is said to be in the anti-LIDAR camp).

Putting aside the LIDAR aspect, take things at face value that the Tesla's are loaded with various sensors and they have specialized AI-related software seeking to undertake self-driving.

Today, for all that's been shown, this rises to a Level 2.

The dribs and drabs of additional self-driving features are perhaps inching the Tesla toward a Level 3.

By his own admission, Elon continues to state that the Tesla cars will still require an attentive and at-the-ready human driver in the car and at the wheel.

Can you reasonably refer to a Level 2 or even a Level 3 car as being superhuman?

It seems like a stretch.

Someday, maybe, when Tesla's are perhaps able to achieve Level 4 or Level 5, which we don't yet know that the existing set of sensors are going to be sufficient to achieve, would that be a time to say they are superhuman?

Presumably, if the same set of sensors as used today are able to via AI be able to perform in a fully compliant way to be rated as Level 4 or Level 5, one might be tempted to allow the superhuman verbiage to slip into the conversation.

What we don't know though is whether common-sense reasoning is needed to really arrive at Level 4 and Level 5 in a fully measured way and if so, please realize that it would mean that nobody has a true self-driving car on the horizon, since AI that embodies common-sense reasoning of a human caliber is still a mere dream.

Conclusion

All in all, rather than having to debate the merits of assigning a superhuman quality to AI, maybe we ought to all agree to stop using the superhuman signature.

In fact, and though realizing that it might be an ego-crushing let down for some, if we can achieve AI that can "merely" do the same things as a human, being able to embody the equivalent intelligence of humans, it would be an awe-inspiring accomplishment of a herculean stature.

Such an AI system might not be super or above our human capacities, but it would incredibly have achieved an immense goal that can only be described as super-tough and super-duper as accomplished by mankind.

Unless, of course, the AI gains singularity and opts to crush all humanity (for more about AI conspiracy theories), in which case, it won't matter whether we perchance called it superhuman since we'll all be washed away.

Say, maybe the AI will actually save all of humanity, and we'll honor it by obliging it with the superhuman title.

I'd be okay with that.

.

CHAPTER 9
SOCIAL DISTANCING AND
AI SELF-DRIVING CARS

CHAPTER 9

SOCIAL DISTANCING AND AI SELF-DRIVING CARS

When you get behind the wheel of your car and go for a leisurely drive, you become an estimator of probabilities whether you realize it or not.

How so?

Driving down your neighborhood street, you might spy a dog that's meandering off its leash.

Assuming that you are a conscientious driver (I hope so!), you would right away start to consider the chances or probabilities that the dog might decide to head into the street.

Presumably, you aren't going to just wildly gauge the odds of the dog doing so, and instead will use some amount of logical reasoning in making your estimation.

For example, you might look to see if the dog is heading away from the street, toward the street, or paralleling the street, plus carefully observe the pace of the pooch.

Meanwhile, you might be considering the speed of your car as it is rolling along, and be judging the timing of when the car could reach the point that the dog might startlingly end-up in your path, assuming that the dog decides to dart out into the street.

Maybe you perchance spot the owner of the dog and realize there's another possibility involved, namely that the owner might realize that a car is going to potentially jeopardize their beloved pet, and perhaps the owner will call out to the dog to get it to retreat away from the impending danger, urging the canine to scamper away from the curb.

Here's a twist on top of it all.

You know the dog, having seen it around and petted it from time-to-time.

Is there a chance that the dog will see you, sitting in the driver's seat, and because of your friendly attachment, it might decide to intentionally come toward the vehicle?

On the other hand, you know that the dog has lived on the block for many years, and never had any incidents with cars, thus, in your mind, you would rate the probability pretty low that the dog will opt to do so now.

Yet, as they say, you never know, this might be the one time that it happens.

Overall, there are seemingly numerous and complex innate probability calculations going on in your noggin about this evolving situation.

Consider this base set of mental machinations and estimations involved:

- What is the probability that the dog will turn toward the street and enter into the roadway (let's label that as the probability of event E occurring)?

- What is the probability that the dog will do so at a timing that would potentially intersect with your car (let's label that as the probability of event I occurring)?

- What is the probability that you will realize the dog is ending up in the street and that you will have sufficient time to hit the brakes to avoid ramming into the animal (label this as the probability of event T)?

- What is the probability that your car will respond to your wishes, namely that if you do have to jam down on your brake pedal that the car brakes will work properly and bring the car to a halt (let's say this is the probability of event H)?

- And so on.

Each of those are specific potential events or occurrences, and each has its own chance or probability of happening, meaning that you've somehow got to come up with a semblance of the probabilities associated with the occurrence of I, E, T, and H.

Furthermore, not only are you estimating those distinct or individual probabilities, you are combining them together to guide your actions as the driver of the car (trying to blend or unite together I, E, T, and H, overall), including coping with those events that are independent of each other and those that are dependent upon each other.

Wow, that's a lot to consider!

Before I proceed with further explanation on the car driving probabilities aspects, let's all assume that you judged wisely and fortunately avoided the pup, which it turned out became so preoccupied with a nearby fire hydrant that it never did get into the way of your car, thankfully.

The overarching point is that you had to make judgments or assessments that involved probabilities.

Thinking About The Thinking Of Probabilities

Some of you might right away be protesting that you drive a car all the time and never need to mathematically make such arcane calculations.

In other words, you insist that your mind is not somehow identifying a numeric value for the likelihood of an event, nor that you are using some complex formula to combine together the probabilities of numerous potential events as though trying to arrive at an overall probabilistic score.

Maybe you don't.

Or, maybe you do, and you just don't realize that you are doing so.

Unlike the probabilities that you might have learned in school, admittedly your mind might not be converting the things you see and do into a numerical description that consists of a probability value between 0 and 1, whereby 0 means the chances are nil of the event occurring and the vaunted value of 1 means it is an absolute certainty.

Furthermore, your thinking processes might not be overtly ascertaining the Merriam-Webster definition of probability, to wit "the ratio of the number of outcomes in an exhaustive set of equally likely outcomes that produce a given event to the total number of possible outcomes."

For those of you that have taken a statistics class, you might recall "fondly" the oft taught Bayes' theorem or rule, named after its author, Thomas Bayes, and his famous formula or algorithm that has to do with conditional probabilities.

Not wanting to stir nightmares of your having taken a mandatory class on stats that maybe didn't go so well for you, but you might recall that you can figure out the probability of an event A occurring given that event B is true, doing so by multiplying the probability of B given A is true, times the probability of A, and dividing that multiplied result by the probability of B.

Or, something like that (go ahead and look it up, you'll smile at the refresher, undoubtedly).

Anyway, let's say that your mind doesn't use those formalized means to calculate probabilities.

For all we know, your mind uses some other approach to deal with probabilities.

Nobody can say for sure.

Our minds are one of the greatest hidden mysteries, locked away in our brain, and within seemingly easy reach, yet remains incredibly inscrutable, despite modern attempts by cognitive scientists, psychology researchers, neuroscientists, and others.

The use of mathematical models such as Bayes's law is useful nonetheless and appears to capture human behavior, which is exhibited by what we do, regardless of what actually takes place via the neurons in the brain.

Contextual Changes In Probabilistic Thinking

In describing the car driving example about the dog, you might have noticed that I purposely indicated that you were taking a leisurely drive.

Imagine how your mind must be racing with probabilities when you are driving under pressure, such as driving on the freeway, in the rain, on the way to work, and you are late and trying to make up for the lost time by driving aggressively.

What happens to your probability estimations then?

It would appear that drivers might adjust their belief about probabilities, based on the context of the driving situation. Since you are late to work, you might mentally justify going past the speed limit and reduce your personal assessment of the probability of getting into a wreck, simply to rationalize your bad driving behavior.

Or, you might think to yourself that you are normally a careful driver, one that takes little or no chances, so you've "earned" the right to drive recklessly, this one time, and are willing to take the chances of getting into a car accident, though you convince yourself the odds are low due to your usually being overall precautious as a driver.

In the United States alone, Americans drive about 3.2 trillion miles per year, which is a lot of miles.

Much of the time, we manage to drive without incident.

This almost seems like a miracle, when you consider that having about 225 million licensed drivers taking to the roads for trillions of miles is bound to be a scary thing. Regrettably, sadly, our driving actions aren't always incident-free, including that there are about 40,000 deaths annually in the U.S. and around 2.5 million injuries due to car crashes.

Speaking of driving, let's consider what is taking place to try and develop AI-based true self-driving cars.

True self-driving cars are ones that can drive without the need for a human driver. The AI system is able to drive the car, and never need to ask assistance from a human driver, and nor require that a human driver is at the wheel and ready to take over the vehicle.

Developing an AI system that can be fully autonomous when driving a car is a lot harder than it might seem.

An ongoing debate involves the role of probabilities.

How so?

Well, recall that we've just discussed that human drivers seem to make use of probabilities, though whether it is a numeric value or some other means of mental consideration is an open question.

Today, we don't require human drivers to explicitly say what probabilities they are using as they drive a car.

We let your actions speak for your words.

If you remain incident-free, apparently you are doing well at your probability estimations. When you get into a car crash, we question your probability thinking and you can potentially go to jail or suffer financial penalties for your driving results.

Consider these crucial questions about an AI self-driving car:

- When building or developing an AI system, and especially one that drives a car, should the AI have explicitly programmed capabilities at probability estimation, such that we can all open the kimono and discuss what probabilities it is using for making life-or-death driving decisions?

- Or, do we let the AI system have hidden assumptions about the probabilities involved in driving, and for which we as humans might not even know or be able to ferret out those encoded probabilities?

The advent of Machine Learning (ML) and Deep Learning (DL) is a handy means to aid in the effort toward "programming" AI systems to drive, yet this also generally is taking us down the path of not being able to explain or articulate what kinds of probabilities are associated with the AI driving system under-the-hood.

In a typical use of ML/DL, you collect lots of data and have the ML/DL algorithms do pattern matching, attempting to identify computationally any underlying patterns. The resulting ML/DL can become large and convoluted, reducing the chances of being able to decipher any logical basis for why the mathematical patterns arise.

How does this relate to the probability of driving?

Suppose I collect lots of driving data associated with human drivers and use that as the primary input into an ML/DL.

The ML/DL tries to model the driving behavior, and then the AI system will drive in a similar manner.

If the data collected was based on say aggressive New York City drivers, presumably the AI system would then have a tendency to drive in a similar vein, based upon the patterns of how those drivers tend to cut corners and take heightened risks while driving.

Digging into the ML/DL model might not especially showcase the matter, and only once the AI system is driving a car, would you begin to realize that the AI has adopted those in-your-face driving tactics.

In short, should AI-based self-driving cars be able to exist and drive on our public roadways even if we can't discern their internal probabilities aspects, allowing them to be opaque or impervious as we allow for the hidden mysteries of what's going on in human minds of drivers, or should we instead insist that the AI systems have to be opened up and reveal explicitly those matters?

Time will tell and so will the public and regulators, depending upon how the AI self-driving car adoptions proceed.

Social Distancing and Probabilities

Recently, we've all suddenly become a lot more conscious about probabilities, though not in the context of driving.

The context now involves social distancing.

To avoid potentially getting infected and to try and curtail or mitigate the rapid spread of the COVID-19 virus, social distancing has become a key tool toward fighting the pandemic.

You might be puzzled about the role of probabilities since it doesn't seem to be an explicit discussion topic when it comes to social distancing.

Well, once again, whether you know it or not, you are indeed making use of probabilities, albeit not necessarily in a formalized mathematical way and instead perhaps in a more instinctive and intuitive manner.

Let's see how.

The rule-of-thumb about contact with others involves remaining at least six feet away.

This is really a physical distancing aspect, rather than a "social" distancing aspect, and some wish that the phrase hadn't become known as social distancing versus say physical distancing. They mention this facet since you can still presumably be sociable in our society, and do so with an added physical distance involved, rather than the sour implication of somehow becoming "anti-social" via distancing yourself from other humans.

In any case, the basis for keeping six feet away from others is due to the attempt to avoid getting the virus on you.

For example:

- If a person has the virus and they physically touch you, there's a chance or probability that they might transfer the virus to you.

- If a person has the virus and coughs or sneezes, there's a chance or probability that the virus now is in the air, and it could land on you.

To try and avoid getting touched by a person that has the virus, you prudently want to stay away from the person, and though you could potentially get within a closer distance and avoid being touched per se, there are the chances too of the airborne form of physical contact, so it makes sense to remain far enough away from the person that the odds of the airborne contact are lessened too.

As a result, society has collectively agreed on a distance of six feet.

It's an easy rule to remember.

Some though misinterpret the rule.

They think it somehow gives them a kind of ironclad guarantee or absolute certainty.

It's more of a rule-of-thumb based on probabilities.

The probability of not physically touching a person that has the virus and that is six feet away from you is considered better than if you were within six feet, and the same is said of the airborne transmission, namely that by staying six feet away you are lowering your probability of having an airborne release of the virus be able to land on you.

Similar to when thinking about a self-driving car or even a human that's driving a car, there are various potential events or occurrences that you are assigning a probability toward when practicing social distancing, such as:

- Probability that a person near you has the virus (let's label this as probability V).

- Probability that the person will make contact with you via touch or via the transmission of their airborne release (let's label this as probability R).

- Probability that once the virus has landed on you that you will contract an infection from the virus (label this as probability C).

- Probability that upon contracting the infection that it will engage your body and cause substantive harm to you (label this as probability Y).

- And so on.

In the case of probability V, we are right now all adopting the perspective that we must assume that V is high for everyone around us, even though we might not know whether that's really the case or not (this has especially become a concern upon the realization that people can have the virus and yet are not displaying any obvious indication, i.e., they can be asymptomatic).

Those college students that seemed to be frolicking in the sun during a Florida spring break, despite the pandemic, could be said to have been underestimating the probabilities involved in this matter (though, some might argue they weren't considering the probabilities altogether or were ill-informed about the probabilities).

If someone falsely believes that Y is near zero, in other words, those that think they are invulnerable and cannot be harmed, the other probabilities of V, R, and C, don't especially matter to them.

Taking precautions such as wearing a mask or face covering are intended to reduce the probability of C, meaning that by putting on a shield or some other precautionary artifact, you are attempting to cut down the chances of C occurring.

For people that go for a stroll or wander around where other people are, they are inextricably going to be mentally coping with probabilities as it pertains to social distancing, whether they realize they are doing so or not. Similar somewhat to the act of driving a car, the situation of the moment will cause you to adjust your perceived probabilities associated with V, R, C, and Y.

Conclusion

Social distancing is a probabilistic based approach.

People are continuously estimating the probabilities associated with encountering other people and having to adjust often on-the-fly as to the perceived risks involved.

When discussing probabilities, it is important to also realize that it is not just the events to consider, but also the consequences or severity of the event itself, assuming that the event does occur.

Events that entail life-or-death consequences require that we be even better at our probability estimations, and the more that people are aware of the matter, hopefully, the more prudent they will be.

CHAPTER 10

APOLLO 13 LESSONS

AND

AI SELF-DRIVING CARS

CHAPTER 10
APOLLO 13 LESSONS AND AI SELF-DRIVING CARS

Time to go on a mission.

There will be important lessons, I promise.

Go back in time to April 11, 1970.

The Apollo 13 mission to the moon was launched from Kennedy Space Center on that date.

Americans and the world had already become somewhat inured about going to the moon, having exalted in the Apollo 11 lunar landing and subsequently gotten used to the "mundaneness" of moonwalks as a result of the success of Apollo 12 (yes, it landed on the moon too!). Alas, not many can recite off the top of their head anything about the Apollo 12 mission, other than that it essentially proved that Apollo 11 wasn't a fluke occurrence.

For Apollo 13, if all went well, the odds are that today we would not be discussing the journey since it would have been "just" another trip to the moon.

April 13, 1970, changed that historical trajectory altogether.

Let's briefly amble through the crucial moments of that fateful April 13.

The date was the 13th and the flight number was 13, a worrisome qualm by some that it might end-up being unlucky (also, if you add together the digits of the launch date 04-11-70, it comes to the number 13, so plenty of reasons to feel potentially bad vibes).

The crew made a TV broadcast at approximately 55 hours into the flight on April 13, 1970, yet few watched because the major broadcast networks decided to run their usual programming instead.

Here's a number to commit to memory: 55:54:53.

That was the exact time at which the mission to the moon became a mission of saving the lives of the astronauts.

About a minute or so earlier, the Houston-based Mission Control had asked Jack Swigert to "stir" the cryo tanks. These were vital tanks on-board the spacecraft and consisted of two oxygen tanks and two hydrogen tanks, used for a multitude of purposes including providing oxygen to the crew and that also generated necessary electric power to run the flight.

The stirring process was routine, not especially notable per se, and had been anticipated to take place from time-to-time to keep the tanks fresh by the use of built-in fans.

It only took the flip of a switch to stir a tank.

Shortly after flipping the stir switch, an explosive and quite unexpected bang was heard by the crew.

At the timestamp of 55:55:42, the commander of Apollo 13, Captain James Lovell, radioed to earth one of the now most famous lines ever uttered from outer space: "Houston, we've had a problem."

Of course, today there are more memes with that quote than you can shake a stick at.

In a nutshell, there was an explosion that arose in the tank, blowing out various other key aspects of the spacecraft and putting the astronauts into a dire situation.

The popular movie starring Tom Hanks about Apollo 13 rather accurately and dramatically depicts the harrowing efforts that followed upon the heels of the spacecraft internal explosion.

One aspect that gets special attention in the movie involved the need to on-the-fly figure out a means to deal with the carbon dioxide that began to accumulate inside the spacecraft (this would have ultimately knocked-out the astronauts and killed them with carbon dioxide poisoning). NASA engineers on earth were tasked with figuring out how to deal with getting gas filtering canisters to fit into a special vent and were limited to only using items that already were on-board the flight.

Little chance of finding a handy-dandy hardware store floating in the outskirts of space.

A makeshift approach that involved using the covers torn from the on-board operations manuals, and using duct tape (proof once again of the heralded worth of duct tape), along with various other items, was devised and then radioed as instructions up to the crew.

The crew embraced the improvisation and fortunately, it worked.

A lot of other equally exciting and hair-raising moments occurred on that flight.

Americans and the world became obsessed with the status of Apollo 13 and no one breathed a sigh of relief until the safe splashdown occurred in the South Pacific.

The splashdown happened on April 17, 1970.

For those of you that want to celebrate the 50th anniversary of the event, you can use either April 11 (official launch date), April 13 (date of the incident occurring), or April 17 (safe splashdown), though most would officially say that the mission start date is the proper date to be used.

Use whichever date you prefer and relish in the valuable lessons learned.

Besides the obvious heroism, there are lots of other keen insights to be gleaned.

The crew and ground control worked as a team, each carefully and thoughtfully coordinating with each other.

Score a point for the value of teamwork.

They all worked systematically and didn't lose their heads, which would have been easy to do, given that the lives of the astronauts were on-the-line. Furthermore, you could reasonably deduce that the future of the moon missions was on-the-line too since the public might have decided "enough is enough" that if the crew was lost then there would not be any more desire to undertake additional flights.

Score a point for being level-headed and steady.

The issue of the canisters was one of many such problems that arose during the return to earth, all of which were step-by-step solved. Most of the arcane problems were not ones that had been previously considered, though a slew of contingency plans had been prepared and practiced.

Score a point for ingenuity and innovation.

For those and other related reasons, it is fair to describe the Apollo 13 as a "successful failure."

The failure aspect has to do with the scrubbing of the moon landing, thus failing to undertake the intended mission.

The success aspect has to do with having been able to deal with a dicey situation that easily could have wiped out the spacecraft and its occupants.

Some take umbrage at calling the mission a "failure" since no one died, and notably, they all came home safe and sound.

Anyway, let's shift gears and consider a different perspective entirely about the Apollo 13 mission.

How did the explosion in the tank occur and what does that showcase, if anything?

Lessons From How It Was Setup

Few of the public know how a series of events led up to the innocuous "ticking timebomb" that the offending tank portended for the mission.

As a backdrop about what I'm about to describe, there's a popular allegory called the Upstream Parable, asserting that our attention is often at downstream events and we don't realize that something upstream led to the calamity in the first place. This makes sense in that when you are trying to solve a problem, you are usually intensely focused on the matter at hand, the downstream crisis, and can't afford to contend with how it came to be (the upstream).

Ultimately, it is usually advantageous to look upstream.

In the case of the tank that exploded, you have to go back in time, quite a while before the Apollo 13 mission took place.

When the tank was first made, it was destined to go on Apollo 10.

Believe it or not, according to a NASA investigation, and per the remarks by Jim Lovell in a fascinating interview for the 50th anniversary, the tank was essentially dropped by the maker of the tank (while on a shelf), suffering internal damage.

A series of follow-on aspects pretty much doomed the tank to become a kind of ticking timebomb. The details are rather technical and intricate, so please do refer to the interview of Lovell or the NASA investigative report if you want those particulars.

In short, here's what happened as a rough chronological set of key actions:

- There was an initial error, which was the dropping of the tank.

- An attempt was made to see if the tank still functioned properly, but this attempt was not comprehensive, and some key functionality was not tested to ensure it still worked. The decision was made to proceed with using the tank, opting to do so for the Apollo 13 mission rather than Apollo 10.

- Prior to the Apollo 13 mission, a countdown demonstration test that included the tank showcased that the tank wouldn't drain as normally expected. Inadvertently, a wrong guess was made as to why the tank wouldn't drain appropriately, and so an alternative method was used to drain it, but this was the "coup de grace" that primed the tank to become a grave danger.

- Though the tank could have been replaced, it would have caused a significant delay in the launch, on the order of reported months, so the decision was made to proceed with it, since it otherwise seemed to be working.

- Just before launch, the tank was filled with liquid oxygen, and at that point, once it was connected to the electrical system, a modest spark such as an electric arc could set the tank on fire and lead to an explosion (note that undamaged tanks would not have been so susceptible).

- The ticking timebomb was then loaded onto the Apollo 13 flight and awaited the moment when something untoward might occur, such as the ill-fated stirring of the tank by Jack Swigert that appeared to cause a spark and detonated the tank, though Swigert had no means of knowing that all of these other series of events had occurred beforehand and would put them all on the brink of upheaval.

Quite a story and a relatively hidden series of seemingly "uneventful" events.

I say "uneventful' since over the course of the thousands of things done to get ready for an activity of this magnitude, it was undoubtedly one tiny thread of the myriad of tasks and subtasks and not one that anyone at the time would have given outstretched special or undue attention toward.

Interesting, you might say, but otherwise what do you care about some oxygen tank that was made and dropped?

Let's dig into the lessons.

First, there was an initial error made, the dropping of the tank.

That's obviously bad, and in itself is a kind of lesson, don't bust things that weren't intended to be busted.

Second, the initial error was compounded by the lack of fully and properly-being tested to ensure that the tank worked as intended.

This can apply to any situation whereby an initial error occurs, and unfortunately, a lack of trying to resolve or fix the error fully is performed.

A half-baked fix is likely to be insidious.

Why?

Because those that know there was a problem will hence believe the problem has been fixed, and won't seek to solve the problem since they believe falsely it has been solved.

Contorted logic, perhaps, but true.

If no one tried to fix it at all, and if it was known that it might have an error, those of a consciousness nature would keep it on the list of things to deal with, eventually either fixing it or deciding it ought to be discarded entirely.

But, by a half-baked fix, those that are involved falsely think it was in fact fixed, and are lulled into believing that the item is now ready for prime time.

Insidious, as I said.

Third, once the tank was being readied for the mission, its reluctance to drain was another potential moment that someone could have realized that things were afoot.

Partially due to the complexity of the components within the tank, those involved postulated a theory about what might be amiss, and thus there was another kind of approach taken (a wrong approach), which seemed to lead to a proper outcome, but actually was making things worse and worse inside the tank.

Thus, this third lesson is that sometimes the complexity overrides our abilities to consider all avenues, and probably under the pressures of the moment, there was less openness to take a step back and rethink the matter.

The fourth lesson is that the astronauts relied on the systems and subsystems of the craft and assumed that they would work as intended, which, certainly makes sense, since how else could you carry on an operation of this magnitude without assuming that everyone else did their jobs properly?

You'd pretty much have little choice but to hope and pray that everyone else did their job.

As a recap of the key lessons:
a) Don't make initial errors
b) Once an initial error is made, don't half-bake a fix
c) Complexities sometimes make it hard to figure out a fix or know that a fix worked
d) The end-user of a system is generally at the mercy of those that made the system

There are other lessons embedded in the saga, but those will be sufficient for the purposes herein.

Applying The Lessons To AI Systems

Those lessons are all applicable to AI systems.

And, especially to large-scale and complex AI systems.

Thus, I implore all AI developers, please heed the lessons, and likewise, the same is true of all companies that are building and fielding AI systems.

What do I mean?

When crafting an AI system, it is easy to potentially make a subtle error inside the coding of the system (see my discussion of the famous go-to-fail coding error that undermined an entire system by a mere syntax misplacement, see the link here).

This includes whether you are crafting a system via conventional coding, whether say in a programming language like Python, C++, LISP, or whatever you might be using.

For those of you using Machine Learning (ML) and Deep Learning (DL), don't assume that if perchance you are using an ML/DL package that does the work of "programming" that you are somehow off-the-hook.

The nature of the data that you used to train the ML/DL might be deficient and lead to an "error" within the ML/DL system that is not at first apparent.

Once made apparent, you could readily try to "solve" the issue by doing a half-baked fix, such as deciding that if the data contained anomalies that led to the issue, you'll just cut out the anomalous data and be done with it.

Unfortunately, it could be that the oddball data was actually a telltale sign of a so-called corner or edge cases that your ML/DL should be handling, and yet ironically, you've now excised out those telltale signals.

Per the lessons about Apollo 13, you might then believe you fixed the problem, and convey this to others, all of whom will then cross-off the issue as no longer needing any attention.

Meanwhile, the ticking timebomb has been set.

For AI systems that perhaps do mundane actions, the error and its consequent carryforward might not be disastrous.

Consider though a life-or-death AI system such as an AI-based self-driving car.

Suppose there are some initial errors inside the AI that sits on-board a self-driving car and that autonomously operates the car controls.

Imagine that at the early testing stage, perhaps while the AI was being used on self-driving cars tested on a special test track or closed-loop course, the issues arose, and under the pressures at the time, the AI team did a half-baked fix.

The self-driving car seemed to continue unabated.

Approval was given to then proceed with trials on public roadways.

You might be thinking that as long as the public roadway trials have a human driver in the vehicle as a safety monitor, being ready to take over the controls, it doesn't matter that the half-baked fix exists. Realize though that perhaps the error is something that only will arise in a blue moon, a rarity, and the number of miles being driven on public roadways might not be sufficient to reach that particular set of errors.

It could be that the public roadway trials seem to go swimmingly, and thus a green light is given to proceed without any human monitor involved. At some point, that lurking error is sitting there and going to be reached, leading potentially to a life-or-death moment for the passengers and for any nearby pedestrians.

Some say that, well, we've got the use of OTA (Over-The-Air) electronic communications capabilities to download patches into the AI system to fix any errors.

Though that might be the case, it's somewhat like trying to corral the horse after it has already gotten out of the barn.

In other words, suppose the self-driving car gets into a car wreck, injuring or killing someone, and only then would the search for the error take place.

Meanwhile, it could be that all of the models of that AI self-driving car have the same embedded error, a ticking timebomb, until the point at which the AI developers figure out what the issue is, come up with a reliable and fully-baked fix, and then push it out to all of the fleet of that AI self-driving car maker.

Conclusion

No matter whether you are building a complex AI system or a simple one, your chances of having some kind of "initial errors" is relatively substantive and serious.

Regrettably, in the pell-mell rush to shove fancy AI systems out-the-door, and with the time pressures and sometimes make-or-break-a-company pressures, there is not as much bona fide software engineering taking place.

As AI systems continue to proliferate, and as they become increasingly used by all of us, we become like the astronaut that merely wanted to flip a switch, expecting that the system had been properly and appropriately devised and fielded.

Surprises such as a catastrophic failure are not an option.

AI, we have a problem, and it is up to AI developers and AI providers to ensure a smooth flight and safe passage.

.

CHAPTER 11
FUTURELAW AND AI SELF-DRIVING CARS

CHAPTER 11

FUTURELAW

AND

AI SELF-DRIVING CARS

William Orville Douglas, an Associate Justice of the U.S. Supreme Court from 1939 to 1975, famously indicated in 1948 that: "The law is not a series of calculating machines where definitions and answers come tumbling out when the right levers are pushed."

As his point vividly suggests, when it comes to law and the practice of law, there is a great deal of human reasoning involved, far beyond the reach of any simplistic calculating machine.

Of course, his authoritative remark was proffered in the late 1940s when computers were massive in size and minuscule in computational capabilities when compared to the power of today's computing, thus an intriguing present-day question is whether the more sophisticated tech and AI systems emerging might someday be able to perform legal tasks on par with that of humans.

A recent conference entitled *FutureLaw 2020* provided an in-depth exploration of the ways that technology is transforming the law, along with the implications for how we will ultimately interact with legal institutions as a result of advances in legal systems.

This annual conference brings together topnotch legal experts from all realms, encompassing academics, research scholars, entrepreneurs, investors, lawyers, regulators, engineers, and the like. Due to the timing coinciding this year with the social distancing efforts underway to cope with the pandemic, the conference was switched into becoming an online virtual collection of videos and podcasts and has been posted for ready access online.

Organized and undertaken by the Stanford Center for Legal Informatics, known generally as CodeX, Dr. Roland Vogl provided an overview of FutureLaw 2020 in his capacity as Executive Director of CodeX and of the Stanford Program in Law, Science and Technology.

CodeX has an emphasis on the research and development of Computational Law.

As stated by Stanford's Professor Michael Genesereth in his excellent paper entitled *Computational Law: The Cop In The Backseat:* "Computational Law is that branch of legal informatics concerned with the codification of regulations in precise, computable form. From a pragmatic perspective, Computational Law is important as the basis for computer systems capable of doing useful legal calculations, such as compliance checking, legal planning, regulatory analysis, and so forth."

As a quick taste of the FutureLaw 2020 sessions, I'll cover next some of the talks that especially raise key AI-related facets, meanwhile generally urging too that you take a further look at the additional videos and podcasts of this stellar collection.

Panel Session: *Is Law's Moat Evaporating?: Implications of Recent NLP Breakthroughs*

Panelists:
Laura Safdie, COO, and General Counsel, Casetext
Khalid Al-Kofahi, VP R&D Thomson Reuters
Daniel Hoadley, Head of Design and Research, ICLR
Anne Tucker, Professor of Law, Georgia State University

This panel covered aspects of advances in Natural Language Processing (NLP), considered one of the tools or capabilities under the overarching umbrella of AI technologies.

On a daily basis, you are bound to find yourself in the midst of NLP, perhaps interacting with Alex or Siri, or maybe you use a chatbot when placing an online order. NLP keeps getting better, becoming more seemingly fluent in interaction and less clunky than prior versions.

During the FutureLaw 2020 session, among various NLP topics covered, the impact of Google's BERT was discussed.

BERT is an NLP software program that is used by Google as part of their search engine efforts and aids in trying to interpret search queries to best find appropriate search results.

What makes BERT a step forward in NLP consists of its approach to examining not just words adjacent to other words in a query, but it also considers the surrounding words. Simpler NLP algorithms tend to only look at each adjacent word, and often parse an entered query on a strictly left-to-right sequence basis, rather than going in a bi-directional manner of scanning both from left-to-right and via right-to-left.

The acronym BERT stands for Bidirectional Encoder Representations from Transformers and attempts to bidirectionally identify the nature or representation of the words used in a query, doing so in a context-based manner. Some refer to BERT as a deep search engine, partially due to the aspect that it is shaped around the use of a deep artificial neural network and uses facets of Machine Learning (ML) and Deep Learning (DL).

Google has made BERT available in an open-source format for those that would like to incorporate the NLP capability into their own apps (various provisions apply to the open-source code usage).

In terms of the law, NLP continues to be added to LegalTech and LawTech systems, allowing for more ready access to volumes of legal documents that otherwise "lock away" vast amounts of potentially crucial legal information but for which human scrutiny alone would not easily be able to find and surface.

Could the advancement of NLP lead to AI that can autonomously do all of your legal research for you?

The panel tackled this thorny question and wrestled with potential timeframes under which AI might reach such a vaunted goal.

It is generally believed that AI will hopefully make the law scale-up or promulgate a future of law-at-scale, meaning that rather than today's law and legal aspects having intractable barriers or hurdles beyond the means of some or many, AI might make the law more readily accessible to all.

Individual Session: *LEX (Law, Education, and Experience) Talks: The Many Faces of Facial Recognition*

Speaker: Stephen Caines, Residential Fellow, CodeX

Facial recognition was at first an amazing and exciting AI breakthrough that the general public found fascinating and handy for seemingly innocuous tasks. Want to get your smartphone to automatically recognize you, doing so without having to manually enter a password, well, just use a built-in facial recognition capability and merely look at your cell phone to get it to open.

Gradually, a realization has emerged that not all is necessarily uplifting about facial recognition.

As noted by expert Stephen Caines in his FutureLaw 2020 session, there are use cases of facial recognition that portend AI-as-good, along with uses that foretell the AI-is-bad side of the AI adoption tradeoffs debates.

He rightfully points out that facial recognition can misidentify people, which if undertaken by a governmental entity could lead to astounding adverse consequences for the public. Furthermore, there is the slippery slope of becoming a surveillance state, whereby initially the impetus was to use facial recognition to nab criminals and then evolves (or devolves) into a Big Brother that ensnares all of us.

Legislative paths toward shaping how facial recognition will be adopted are multi-faceted right now and include some attempts to ban facial recognition in certain contexts and regulate it in other contexts, leading currently toward a myriad of confounding and possibly conflicting approaches.

In discussing the regulatory efforts, Caines urges that we seek to find ways to use facial recognition for well-needed pursuits, such as protecting those in society that are otherwise vulnerable and could benefit by the added protection afforded by facial recognition, and that to see this occur fruitfully and with a proper balance that the onus is on us to take on personal responsibility to get engaged in the formation of local laws and via ongoing contact with our legislative representatives.

Individual Session: *A Conversation About Legal Innovation, AI And Cybersecurity*

Speaker: Brigadier General Patrick Huston, The Pentagon, Assistant Judge Advocate General

In an invigorating Q&A format, moderator Dr. Roland Vogl interacts with Brigadier General Patrick Huston about the intertwining facets of legal innovation, AI, and cybersecurity.

There are a smattering of online videos today that showcase the use of DeepFake AI, wherein a video of a noted celebrity or political figure seems to be saying things that don't comport with what they might have actually said, or in which the head or face of such a notable person is shorn onto the body of someone else.

151

Currently, you can often detect telltale verbal or visual clues that suggest that some form of audio or video trickery was used.

Unfortunately, the DeepFakes are getting more advanced and gradually it will become extremely hard to discern a true audio or video from one that has been transformed via these latest AI techniques and tools.

Brigadier General Patrick includes the foreboding expansion of DeepFakes into the lengthy list of things that lamentably keep him up at night.

As a long-time member of the armed services, along with being a West Point grad and an Army War College alum, some might be surprised to know that he is also a human rights lawyer. He points out that his military service and his devotion to human rights are not somehow at odds with each other, and in fact are complementary to each other.

Besides covering a range of topics such as the existent paradigm shift taking place in how the government develops tech (and the role of the commercial sector), along with pointing out that there isn't some form of magical AI pixie dust that will overnight change our systems and what they do, he stridently emphasizes that we need to keep cybersecurity at the forefront of our thinking on these matters.

I especially appreciated his highlighting the role of cybersecurity since many of those rushing to put AI systems into practice are not seemingly aware of or concerned about how those systems can be cracked or otherwise overturned into performing evildoer tasks, regardless of whether the original intent was for something of an innocent and grandiose desired benefit.

Individual Session: *LEX (Law, Education, and Experience) Talks: VC Investment In Time Of Crisis*

Speaker: David Hornik, Venture Capitalist, August Capital

In this insightful and timely Q&A session with David Hornik, one question on the minds of many is whether Venture Capital (VC) is going to dry up or otherwise shift direction as a result of the pandemic, changing VC practices in the near-term and possibly for the longer term.

It makes a big difference to all those fledgling startups, some that have already gotten a modicum of VC funding and for those too that are fresh startups with a dreamy eye towards getting VC investments.

Per notable venture capitalist David Hornik, in the near-term, startups ought to realize that getting VC funding is going to be a bit more arduous, thus those budding entrepreneurs need to hunker down and try to deal with their existing burn rates, stretching out whatever money they already have in the bank and making do accordingly.

Meanwhile, he points out that he's continuing to push forward on his VC efforts, as are many VC's, given that much of their work can be performed remotely. Those long days at the office have become long days at home, carrying on the continual series of phone calls and online interactions that are part-and-parcel of finding worthwhile startup investments.

In the legal realm and the use of tech, one particularly innovative avenue of AI would consist of using AI to try and predict the pricing for legal services. As anyone in the legal profession knows, there is an ongoing debate about pricing on an hourly basis versus pricing for the case at hand, encompassing tensions whichever way the pricing is ascertained.

Might it be feasible to analyze a large corpus of legal efforts to derive via say Machine Learning or Deep Learning patterns or models that could accurately predict the magnitude of a legal effort as required for a new case about to be started?

It's an interesting proposition.

Speaking of which, when asked about which technologies or AI uses seem to be on his shopping list, Hornik pointed out that he tends to look for entrepreneurs that see transformative or disruptive opportunities, rather than opting for him to pick or choose specific tech advances per se.

This is reminiscent of the classic line in the VC/PE tech arena, namely, do you bet on the horse or on the rider. The horse is the underlying tech, while the rider being the entrepreneur. As seasoned investors know, you are likely better off to bet on the rider, an entrepreneur, one with the spunk and vision for the long haul, and do so since the odds are that they'll find the right opportunities, even if it means pivoting to do so.

AI And Autonomy

Let's further consider some of those insights gleaned from the aforementioned sessions.

Most AI systems today are at best semi-autonomous, and not yet fully autonomous.

AI advances keep pushing toward being able to have an AI system essentially do work on its own.

For example, we are gradually witnessing self-driving cars that are able to proceed on an autonomous basis. There won't be a human driver at the wheel. Nor will a human driver need to be remotely connected to the vehicle to make it operational.

We're not there yet.

Could we also see AI working autonomously in the legal field?

Well, for years there has been an endless parade of claimed robo-lawyers or robot lawyers, suggesting that an AI system can do whatever a human lawyer can do.

Nope, not the case.

As yet.

Do realize that there is a vast difference between autonomously driving a car and autonomously performing the tasks of a human lawyer.

In the handling of law, one deals with text, lots and lots of text, all of which is wide open to interpretation, indeed some lament overly open to interpretation.

One of the grand hurdles of AI as a lawyer involves coping with the *semantically indeterminate* nature of law and the practice of law.

This is a cognitive capability that does not boil down into mechanized rules and procedures, despite the belief by some that all you need to do is write down all the legal rules and voila, you'd have yourself an AI-based autonomous lawyer.

There's more to it.

Some in AI have even flagrantly suggested that the law ought to be changed to fit with what AI can currently do, rather than continuing to try and advance AI to do what the law needs.

This sentiment reminds me of the quote by Montesquieu (1748), in De l'Esprit des Lois: "Thus when a man takes on absolute power, he first thinks of simplifying the law. In such a state one begins to be more affected by technicalities than by the freedom of the people, about which one no longer cares at all."

I don't think we want to start flattening or stifling law simply to make it more amenable to being implemented in AI.

That's a bad idea and would undoubtedly have the sour (and dire) outcomes envisioned by Montesquieu.

AI is going to continue to advance and indubitably expand its encroachment into the law, hopefully, though aiding and enabling human lawyers, and we'll need to keep an eye out for the AI that one-day tips over from being semi-autonomous into autonomous.

A fascinating course at Stanford is taking place this term on AI and the Rule of Law, co-taught by Stanford Professor David Engstrom and by Marietje Schaake, the International Policy Director and International Policy Fellow for Stanford's HAI (Institute for Human-Centered AI), exploring how advances in AI and the like are transforming our world and regulations.

More on their findings in a future piece.

Conclusion

If William Shakespeare were alive today, and if he could revamp his famous line from Henry VI, do you think he might say that the first thing we do, let's transform all the lawyers into AI?

A snarky person might say yes, while a pragmatist might ask how it might be done and what impacts would we experience.

Poetically, it could be the future of law and the future of AI.

APPENDIX

APPENDIX A
TEACHING WITH THIS MATERIAL

The material in this book can be readily used either as a supplemental to other content for a class, or it can also be used as a core set of textbook material for a specialized class. Classes where this material is most likely used include any classes at the college or university level that want to augment the class by offering thought provoking and educational essays about AI and self-driving cars.

In particular, here are some aspects for class use:

o   Computer Science. Studying AI, autonomous vehicles, etc.

o   Business. Exploring technology and it adoption for business.

o   Sociology. Sociological views on the adoption and advancement of technology.

Specialized classes at the undergraduate and graduate level can also make use of this material.

For each chapter, consider whether you think the chapter provides material relevant to your course topic. There is plenty of opportunity to get the students thinking about the topic and force them to decide whether they agree or disagree with the points offered and positions taken. I would also encourage you to have the students do additional research beyond the chapter material presented (I provide next some suggested assignments they can do).

RESEARCH ASSIGNMENTS ON THESE TOPICS

Your students can find background material on these topics, doing so in various business and technical publications. I list below the top ranked AI related journals. For business publications, I would suggest the usual culprits such as the Harvard Business Review, Forbes, Fortune, WSJ, and the like.

Here are some suggestions of homework or projects that you could assign to students:

a) Assignment for foundational AI research topic: Research and prepare a paper and a presentation on a specific aspect of Deep AI, Machine Learning, ANN, etc. The paper should cite at least 3 reputable sources. Compare and contrast to what has been stated in this book.

b) Assignment for the Self-Driving Car topic: Research and prepare a paper and Self-Driving Cars. Cite at least 3 reputable sources and analyze the characterizations. Compare and contrast to what has been stated in this book.

c) Assignment for a Business topic: Research and prepare a paper and a presentation on businesses and advanced technology. What is hot, and what is not? Cite at least 3 reputable sources. Compare and contrast to the depictions in this book.

d) Assignment to do a Startup: Have the students prepare a paper about how they might startup a business in this realm. They must submit a sound Business Plan for the startup. They could also be asked to present their Business Plan and so should also have a presentation deck to coincide with it.

You can certainly adjust the aforementioned assignments to fit to your particular needs and the class structure. You'll notice that I ask for 3 reputable cited sources for the paper writing based assignments. I usually steer students toward "reputable" publications, since otherwise they will cite some oddball source that has no credentials other than that they happened to write something and post it onto the Internet. You can define "reputable" in whatever way you prefer, for example some faculty think Wikipedia is not reputable while others believe it is reputable and allow students to cite it.

The reason that I usually ask for at least 3 citations is that if the student only does one or two citations they usually settle on whatever they happened to find the fastest. By requiring three citations, it usually seems to force them to look around, explore, and end-up probably finding five or more, and then whittling it down to 3 that they will actually use.

I have not specified the length of their papers, and leave that to you to tell the students what you prefer. For each of those assignments, you could end-up with a short one to two pager, or you could do a dissertation length paper. Base the length on whatever best fits for your class, and the credit amount of the assignment within the context of the other grading metrics you'll be using for the class.

I mention in the assignments that they are to do a paper and prepare a presentation. I usually try to get students to present their work. This is a good practice for what they will do in the business world. Most of the time, they will be required to prepare an analysis and present it. If you don't have the class time or inclination to have the students present, then you can of course cut out the aspect of them putting together a presentation.

If you want to point students toward highly ranked journals in AI, here's a list of the top journals as reported by *various citation counts sources* (this list changes year to year):

- o Communications of the ACM
- o Artificial Intelligence
- o Cognitive Science
- o IEEE Transactions on Pattern Analysis and Machine Intelligence
- o Foundations and Trends in Machine Learning
- o Journal of Memory and Language
- o Cognitive Psychology
- o Neural Networks
- o IEEE Transactions on Neural Networks and Learning Systems
- o IEEE Intelligent Systems
- o Knowledge-based Systems

GUIDE TO USING THE CHAPTERS

For each of the chapters, I provide next some various ways to use the chapter material. You can assign the tasks as individual homework assignments, or the tasks can be used with team projects for the class. You can easily layout a series of assignments, such as indicating that the students are to do item "a" below for say Chapter 1, then "b" for the next chapter of the book, and so on.

a) What is the main point of the chapter and describe in your own words the significance of the topic,

b) Identify at least two aspects in the chapter that you agree with, and support your concurrence by providing at least one other outside researched item as support; make sure to explain your basis for disagreeing with the aspects,

c) Identify at least two aspects in the chapter that you disagree with, and support your disagreement by providing at least one other outside researched item as support; make sure to explain your basis for disagreeing with the aspects,

d) Find an aspect that was not covered in the chapter, doing so by conducting outside research, and then explain how that aspect ties into the chapter and what significance it brings to the topic,

e) Interview a specialist in industry about the topic of the chapter, collect from them their thoughts and opinions, and readdress the chapter by citing your source and how they compared and contrasted to the material,

f) Interview a relevant academic professor or researcher in a college or university about the topic of the chapter, collect from them their thoughts and opinions, and readdress the chapter by citing your source and how they compared and contrasted to the material,

g) Try to update a chapter by finding out the latest on the topic, and ascertain whether the issue or topic has now been solved or whether it is still being addressed, explain what you come up with.

The above are all ways in which you can get the students of your class involved in considering the material of a given chapter. You could mix things up by having one of those above assignments per each week, covering the chapters over the course of the semester or quarter.

As a reminder, here are the chapters of the book and you can select whichever chapters you find most valued for your particular class:

Chapter Title

1   Eliot Framework for AI Self-Driving Cars

2   Baby Sea Lion and AI Self-Driving Cars

3   Traffic Lights and AI Self-Driving Cars

4   Roadway Edge Computing and AI Self-Driving Cars

5   Ground Penetrating Radar and AI Self-Driving Cars

6   Upstream Parable and AI Self-Driving Cars

7   Red-Light Auto-Stopping and Self-Driving Cars

8   Falseness of Superhuman AI Self-Driving Cars

9   Social Distancing and AI Self-Driving Cars

10   Apollo 13 Lessons and AI Self-Driving Cars

11   FutureLaw and AI Self-Driving Cars

<u>Companion Book By This Author</u>

Advances in AI and Autonomous Vehicles: Cybernetic Self-Driving Cars

Practical Advances in Artificial Intelligence (AI) and Machine Learning

by

Dr. Lance B. Eliot, MBA, PhD

<u>Chapter Title</u>

1 Genetic Algorithms for Self-Driving Cars

2 Blockchain for Self-Driving Cars

3 Machine Learning and Data for Self-Driving Cars

4 Edge Problems at Core of True Self-Driving Cars

5 Solving the Roundabout Traversal Problem for SD Cars

6 Parallel Parking Mindless Task for SD Cars: Step It Up

7 Caveats of Open Source for Self-Driving Cars

8 Catastrophic Cyber Hacking of Self-Driving Cars

9 Conspicuity for Self-Driving Cars

10 Accident Scene Traversal for Self-Driving Cars

11 Emergency Vehicle Awareness for Self-Driving Cars

12 Are Left Turns Right for Self-Driving Cars

13 Going Blind: When Sensors Fail on Self-Driving Cars

14 Roadway Debris Cognition for Self-Driving Cars

15 Avoiding Pedestrian Roadkill by Self-Driving Cars

16 When Accidents Happen to Self-Driving Cars

17 Illegal Driving for Self-Driving Cars

18 Making AI Sense of Road Signs

19 Parking Your Car the AI Way

20 Not Fast Enough: Human Factors in Self-Driving Cars

21 State of Government Reporting on Self-Driving Cars

22 The Head Nod Problem for Self-Driving Cars

23 CES Reveals Self-Driving Car Differences

This title is available via Amazon and other book sellers

Companion Book By This Author

Self-Driving Cars:
"The Mother of All AI Projects"

by Dr. Lance B. Eliot, MBA, PhD

Chapter Title

1 Grand Convergence Explains Rise of Self-Driving Cars

2 Here is Why We Need to Call Them Self-Driving Cars

3 Richter Scale for Levels of Self-Driving Cars

4 LIDAR as Secret Sauce for Self-Driving Cars

5 Pied Piper Approach to SD Car-Following

6 Sizzle Reel Trickery for AI Self-Driving Car Hype

7 Roller Coaster Public Perception of Self-Driving Cars

8 Brainless Self-Driving Shuttles Not Same as SD Cars

9 First Salvo Class Action Lawsuits for Defective SD Cars

10 AI Fake News About Self-Driving Cars

11 Rancorous Ranking of Self-Driving Cars

12 Product Liability for Self-Driving Cars

13 Humans Colliding with Self-Driving Cars

14 Elderly Boon or Bust for Self-Driving Cars

15 Simulations for Self-Driving Cars: Machine Learning

16 DUI Drunk Driving by Self-Driving Cars

17 Ten Human-Driving Foibles: Deep Learning

18 Art of Defensive Driving is Key to Self-Driving Cars

19 Cyclops Approach to AI Self-Driving Cars is Myopic

20 Steering Wheel Gets Self-Driving Car Attention

21 Remote Piloting is a Self-Driving Car Crutch

22 Self-Driving Cars: Zero Fatalities, Zero Chance

23 Goldrush: Self-Driving Car Lawsuit Bonanza Ahead

24 Road Trip Trickery for Self-Driving Trucks and Cars

25 Ethically Ambiguous Self-Driving Car

This title is available via Amazon and other book seller

Innovation and Thought Leadership on Self-Driving Driverless Cars

by Dr. Lance B. Eliot, MBA, PhD

Chapter Title

1 Sensor Fusion for Self-Driving Cars

2 Street Scene Free Space Detection Self-Driving Cars

3 Self-Awareness for Self-Driving Cars

4 Cartographic Trade-offs for Self-Driving Cars

5 Toll Road Traversal for Self-Driving Cars

6 Predictive Scenario Modeling for Self-Driving Cars

7 Selfishness for Self-Driving Cars

8 Leap Frog Driving for Self-Driving Cars

9 Proprioceptive IMU's for Self-Driving Cars

10 Robojacking of Self-Driving Cars

11 Self-Driving Car Moonshot and Mother of AI Projects

12 Marketing of Self-Driving Cars

13 Are Airplane Autopilots Same as Self-Driving Cars

14 Savvy Self-Driving Car Regulators: Marc Berman

15 Event Data Recorders (EDR) for Self-Driving Cars

16 Looking Behind You for Self-Driving Cars

17 In-Car Voice Commands NLP for Self-Driving Cars

18 When Self-Driving Cars Get Pulled Over by a Cop

19 Brainjacking Neuroprosthetus Self-Driving Cars

This title is available via Amazon and other book sellers

Companion Book By This Author

New Advances in AI Autonomous Driverless Cars Self-Driving Cars

by Dr. Lance B. Eliot, MBA, PhD

Chapter Title

1 Eliot Framework for AI Self-Driving Cars

2 Self-Driving Cars Learning from Self-Driving Cars

3 Imitation as Deep Learning for Self-Driving Cars

4 Assessing Federal Regulations for Self-Driving Cars

5 Bandwagon Effect for Self-Driving Cars

6 AI Backdoor Security Holes for Self-Driving Cars

7 Debiasing of AI for Self-Driving Cars

8 Algorithmic Transparency for Self-Driving Cars

9 Motorcycle Disentanglement for Self-Driving Cars

10 Graceful Degradation Handling of Self-Driving Cars

11 AI for Home Garage Parking of Self-Driving Cars

12 Motivational AI Irrationality for Self-Driving Cars

13 Curiosity as Cognition for Self-Driving Cars

14 Automotive Recalls of Self-Driving Cars

15 Internationalizing AI for Self-Driving Cars

16 Sleeping as AI Mechanism for Self-Driving Cars

17 Car Insurance Scams and Self-Driving Cars

18 U-Turn Traversal AI for Self-Driving Cars

19 Software Neglect for Self-Driving Cars

This title is available via Amazon and other book sellers

Companion Book By This Author

Introduction to
Driverless Self-Driving Cars

by Dr. Lance B. Eliot, MBA, PhD

Chapter Title

1   Self-Driving Car Moonshot: Mother of All AI Projects
2   Grand Convergence Leads to Self-Driving Cars
3   Why They Should Be Called Self-Driving Cars
4   Richter Scale for Self-Driving Car Levels
5   LIDAR for Self-Driving Cars
6   Overall Framework for Self-Driving Cars
7   Sensor Fusion is Key for Self-Driving Cars
8   Humans Not Fast Enough for Self-Driving Cars
9   Solving Edge Problems of Self-Driving Cars
10 Graceful Degradation for Faltering Self-Driving Cars
11 Genetic Algorithms for Self-Driving Cars
12 Blockchain for Self-Driving Cars
13 Machine Learning and Data for Self-Driving Cars
14 Cyber-Hacking of Self-Driving Cars
15 Sensor Failures in Self-Driving Cars
16 When Accidents Happen to Self-Driving Cars
17 Backdoor Security Holes in Self-Driving Cars
18 Future Brainjacking for Self-Driving Cars
19 Internationalizing Self-Driving Cars
20 Are Airline Autopilots Same as Self-Driving Cars
21 Marketing of Self-Driving Cars
22 Fake News about Self-Driving Cars
23 Product Liability for Self-Driving Cars
24 Zero Fatalities Zero Chance for Self-Driving Cars
25 Road Trip Trickery for Self-Driving Cars
26 Ethical Issues of Self-Driving Cars
27 Ranking of Self-Driving Cars
28 Induced Demand Driven by Self-Driving Cars

This title is available via Amazon and other book sellers

Companion Book By This Author
Autonomous Vehicle Driverless
Self-Driving Cars and Artificial Intelligence
by Dr. Lance B. Eliot, MBA, PhD

Chapter Title

1 Eliot Framework for AI Self-Driving Cars

2 Rocket Man Drivers and AI Self-Driving Cars

3 Occam's Razor Crucial for AI Self-Driving Cars

4 Simultaneous Local/Map (SLAM) for Self-Driving Cars

5 Swarm Intelligence for AI Self-Driving Cars

6 Biomimicry and Robomimicry for Self-Driving Cars

7 Deep Compression/Pruning for AI Self-Driving Cars

8 Extra-Scenery Perception for AI Self-Driving Cars

9 Invasive Curve and AI Self-Driving Cars

10 Normalization of Deviance and AI Self-Driving Cars

11 Groupthink Dilemma for AI Self-Driving Cars

12 Induced Demand Driven by AI Self-Driving Cars

13 Compressive Sensing for AI Self-Driving Cars

14 Neural Layer Explanations for AI Self-Driving Cars

15 Self-Adapting Resiliency for AI Self-Driving Cars

16 Prisoner's Dilemma and AI Self-Driving Cars

17 Turing Test and AI Self-Driving Cars

18 Support Vector Machines for AI Self-Driving Cars

19 "Expert Systems and AI Self-Driving Cars" by Michael Eliot

This title is available via Amazon and other book sellers

Companion Book By This Author

Transformative Artificial Intelligence Driverless Self-Driving Cars

by Dr. Lance B. Eliot, MBA, PhD

<u>Chapter Title</u>

1   Eliot Framework for AI Self-Driving Cars

2   Kinetosis Anti-Motion Sickness for Self-Driving Cars

3   Rain Driving for Self-Driving Cars

4   Edge Computing for Self-Driving Cars

5   Motorcycles as AI Self-Driving Vehicles

6   CAPTCHA Cyber-Hacking and Self-Driving Cars

7   Probabilistic Reasoning for Self-Driving Cars

8   Proving Grounds for Self-Driving Cars

9   Frankenstein and AI Self-Driving Cars

10 Omnipresence for Self-Driving Cars

11 Looking Behind You for Self-Driving Cars

12 Over-The-Air (OTA) Updating for Self-Driving Cars

13 Snow Driving for Self-Driving Cars

14 Human-Aided Training for Self-Driving Cars

15 Privacy for Self-Driving Cars

16 Transduction Vulnerabilities for Self-Driving Cars

17 Conversations Computing and Self-Driving Cars

18 Flying Debris and Self-Driving Cars

19 Citizen AI for Self-Driving Cars

This title is available via Amazon and other book sellers

**Disruptive Artificial Intelligence
and Driverless Self-Driving Cars**

by Dr. Lance B. Eliot, MBA, PhD

Chapter Title

1 Eliot Framework for AI Self-Driving Cars

2 Maneuverability and Self-Driving Cars

3 Common Sense Reasoning and Self-Driving Cars

4 Cognition Timing and Self-Driving Cars

5 Speed Limits and Self-Driving Vehicles

6 Human Back-up Drivers and Self-Driving Cars

7 Forensic Analysis Uber and Self-Driving Cars

8 Power Consumption and Self-Driving Cars

9 Road Rage and Self-Driving Cars

10 Conspiracy Theories and Self-Driving Cars

11 Fear Landscape and Self-Driving Cars

12 Pre-Mortem and Self-Driving Cars

13 Kits and Self-Driving Cars

This title is available via Amazon and other book sellers

Companion Book By This Author

State-of-the-Art
AI Driverless Self-Driving Cars

by Dr. Lance B. Eliot, MBA, PhD

Chapter Title

1 Eliot Framework for AI Self-Driving Cars

2 Versioning and Self-Driving Cars

3 Towing and Self-Driving Cars

4 Driving Styles and Self-Driving Cars

5 Bicyclists and Self-Driving Vehicles

6 Back-up Cams and Self-Driving Cars

7 Traffic Mix and Self-Driving Cars

8 Hot-Car Deaths and Self-Driving Cars

9 Machine Learning Performance and Self-Driving Cars

10 Sensory Illusions and Self-Driving Cars

11 Federated Machine Learning and Self-Driving Cars

12 Irreproducibility and Self-Driving Cars

13 In-Car Deliveries and Self-Driving Cars

This title is available via Amazon and other book sellers

<u>Companion Book By This Author</u>

Top Trends in
AI Self-Driving Cars

by Dr. Lance B. Eliot, MBA, PhD

<u>Chapter Title</u>

1   Eliot Framework for AI Self-Driving Cars

2   Responsibility and Self-Driving Cars

3   Changing Lanes and Self-Driving Cars

4   Procrastination and Self-Driving Cars

5   NTSB Report and Tesla Car Crash

6   Start Over AI and Self-Driving Cars

7   Freezing Robot Problem and Self-Driving Cars

8   Canarying and Self-Driving Cars

9   Nighttime Driving and Self-Driving Cars

10 Zombie-Cars Taxes and Self-Driving Cars

11 Traffic Lights and Self-Driving Cars

12 Reverse Engineering and Self-Driving Cars

13 Singularity AI and Self-Driving Cars

This title is available via Amazon and other book sellers

Companion Book By This Author

AI Innovations and Self-Driving Cars

by Dr. Lance B. Eliot, MBA, PhD

Chapter Title

1   Eliot Framework for AI Self-Driving Cars

2   API's and Self-Driving Cars

3   Egocentric Designs and Self-Driving Cars

4   Family Road Trip and Self-Driving Cars

5   AI Developer Burnout and Tesla Car Crash

6   Stealing Secrets About Self-Driving Cars

7   Affordability and Self-Driving Cars

8   Crossing the Rubicon and Self-Driving Cars

9   Addicted to Self-Driving Cars

10 Ultrasonic Harm and Self-Driving Cars

11 Accidents Contagion and Self-Driving Cars

12 Non-Stop 24x7 and Self-Driving Cars

13 Human Life Spans and Self-Driving Cars

This title is available via Amazon and other book sellers

Companion Book By This Author

Crucial Advances for
AI Self-Driving Cars

by Dr. Lance B. Eliot, MBA, PhD

Chapter Title

1 Eliot Framework for AI Self-Driving Cars

2 Ensemble Learning and AI Self-Driving Cars

3 Ghost in AI Self-Driving Cars

4 Public Shaming of AI Self-Driving

5 Internet of Things (IoT) and AI Self-Driving Cars

6 Personal Rapid Transit (RPT) and Self-Driving Cars

7 Eventual Consistency and AI Self-Driving Cars

8 Mass Transit Future and AI Self-Driving Cars

9 Coopetition and AI Self-Driving Cars

10 Electric Vehicles (EVs) and AI Self-Driving Cars

11 Dangers of In-Motion AI Self-Driving Cars

12 Sports Cars and AI Self-Driving Cars

13 Game Theory and AI Self-Driving Cars

This title is available via Amazon and other book sellers

Companion Book By This Author

Sociotechnical Insights and AI Driverless Cars

by Dr. Lance B. Eliot, MBA, PhD

Chapter Title

1   Eliot Framework for AI Self-Driving Cars

2   Start-ups and AI Self-Driving Cars

3   Code Obfuscation and AI Self-Driving Cars

4   Hyperlanes and AI Self-Driving Cars

5   Passenger Panic Inside an AI Self-Driving Car

6   Tech Stockholm Syndrome and Self-Driving Cars

7   Paralysis and AI Self-Driving Cars

8   Ugly Zones and AI Self-Driving Cars

9   Ridesharing and AI Self-Driving Cars

10 Multi-Party Privacy and AI Self-Driving Cars

11 Chaff Bugs and AI Self-Driving Cars

12 Social Reciprocity and AI Self-Driving Cars

13 Pet Mode and AI Self-Driving Cars

This title is available via Amazon and other book sellers

Companion Book By This Author

Pioneering Advances for AI Driverless Cars

by Dr. Lance B. Eliot, MBA, PhD

<u>Chapter Title</u>

1   Eliot Framework for AI Self-Driving Cars

2   Boxes on Wheels and AI Self-Driving Cars

3   Clogs and AI Self-Driving Cars

4   Kids Communicating with AI Self-Driving Cars

5   Incident Awareness and AI Self-Driving Car

6   Emotion Recognition and Self-Driving Cars

7   Rear-End Collisions and AI Self-Driving Cars

8   Autonomous Nervous System and AI Self-Driving Cars

9   Height Warnings and AI Self-Driving Cars

10 Future Jobs and AI Self-Driving Cars

11 Car Wash and AI Self-Driving Cars

12 5G and AI Self-Driving Cars

13 Gen Z and AI Self-Driving Cars

This title is available via Amazon and other book sellers

Companion Book By This Author

Leading Edge Trends for AI Driverless Cars

by Dr. Lance B. Eliot, MBA, PhD

Chapter Title

1 Eliot Framework for AI Self-Driving Cars

2 Pranking and AI Self-Driving Cars

3 Drive-Thrus and AI Self-Driving Cars

4 Overworking on AI Self-Driving Cars

5 Sleeping Barber Problem and AI Self-Driving Cars

6 System Load Balancing and AI Self-Driving Cars

7 Virtual Spike Strips and AI Self-Driving Cars

8 Razzle Dazzle Camouflage and AI Self-Driving Cars

9 Rewilding of AI Self-Driving Cars

10 Brute Force Algorithms and AI Self-Driving Cars

11 Idle Moments and AI Self-Driving Cars

12 Hurricanes and AI Self-Driving Cars

13 Object Visual Transplants and AI Self-Driving Cars

This title is available via Amazon and other book sellers

Companion Book By This Author

The Cutting Edge of AI Autonomous Cars

by Dr. Lance B. Eliot, MBA, PhD

Chapter Title

1 Eliot Framework for AI Self-Driving Cars

2 Driving Controls and AI Self-Driving Cars

3 Bug Bounty and AI Self-Driving Cars

4 Lane Splitting and AI Self-Driving Cars

5 Drunk Drivers versus AI Self-Driving Cars

6 Internal Naysayers and AI Self-Driving Cars

7 Debugging and AI Self-Driving Cars

8 Ethics Review Boards and AI Self-Driving Cars

9 Road Diets and AI Self-Driving Cars

10 Wrong Way Driving and AI Self-Driving Cars

11 World Safety Summit and AI Self-Driving Cars

This title is available via Amazon and other book sellers

Companion Book By This Author

The Next Wave of
AI Self-Driving Cars

by Dr. Lance B. Eliot, MBA, PhD

Chapter Title

1 Eliot Framework for AI Self-Driving Cars

2 Productivity and AI Self-Driving Cars

3 Blind Pedestrians and AI Self-Driving Cars

4 Fail-Safe AI and AI Self-Driving Cars

5 Anomaly Detection and AI Self-Driving Cars

6 Running Out of Gas and AI Self-Driving Cars

7 Deep Personalization and AI Self-Driving Cars

8 Reframing the Levels of AI Self-Driving Cars

9 Cryptojacking and AI Self-Driving Cars

This title is available via Amazon and other book sellers

<u>Companion Book By This Author</u>

Revolutionary Innovations of AI Self-Driving Cars

by Dr. Lance B. Eliot, MBA, PhD

<u>Chapter Title</u>

1   Eliot Framework for AI Self-Driving Cars

2   Exascale Supercomputer and AI Self-Driving Cars

3   Superhuman AI and AI Self-Driving Cars

4   Olfactory e-Nose Sensors and AI Self-Driving Cars

5   Perpetual Computing and AI Self-Driving Cars

6   Byzantine Generals Problem and AI Self-Driving Cars

7   Driver Traffic Guardians and AI Self-Driving Cars

8   Anti-Gridlock Laws and AI Self-Driving Cars

9   Arguing Machines and AI Self-Driving Cars

This title is available via Amazon and other book sellers

Companion Book By This Author

AI Self-Driving Cars
Breakthroughs

by Dr. Lance B. Eliot, MBA, PhD

Chapter Title

1   Eliot Framework for AI Self-Driving Cars

2   Off-Roading and AI Self-Driving Cars

3   Paralleling Vehicles and AI Self-Driving Cars

4   Dementia Drivers and AI Self-Driving Cars

5   Augmented Realty (AR) and AI Self-Driving Cars

6   Sleeping Inside an AI Self-Driving Car

7   Prevalence Detection and AI Self-Driving Cars

8   Super-Intelligent AI and AI Self-Driving Cars

9   Car Caravans and AI Self-Driving Cars

This title is available via Amazon and other book sellers

Companion Book By This Author

Trailblazing Trends for **AI Self-Driving Cars**

by Dr. Lance B. Eliot, MBA, PhD

Chapter Title

1   Eliot Framework for AI Self-Driving Cars

2   Strategic AI Metaphors and AI Self-Driving Cars

3   Emergency-Only AI and AI Self-Driving Cars

4   Animal Drawn Vehicles and AI Self-Driving Cars

5   Chess Play and AI Self-Driving Cars

6   Cobots Exoskeletons and AI Self-Driving Car

7   Economic Commodity and AI Self-Driving Cars

8   Road Racing and AI Self-Driving Cars

This title is available via Amazon and other book sellers

Companion Book By This Author

***Ingenious Strides* for
AI Driverless Cars**

by Dr. Lance B. Eliot, MBA, PhD

Chapter Title

1   Eliot Framework for AI Self-Driving Cars

2   Plasticity and AI Self-Driving Cars

3   NIMBY vs. YIMBY and AI Self-Driving Cars

4   Top Trends for 2019 and AI Self-Driving Cars

5   Rural Areas and AI Self-Driving Cars

6   Self-Imposed Constraints and AI Self-Driving Car

7   Alien Limb Syndrome and AI Self-Driving Cars

8   Jaywalking and AI Self-Driving Cars

This title is available via Amazon and other book sellers

Companion Book By This Author

AI Self-Driving Cars
Inventiveness

by Dr. Lance B. Eliot, MBA, PhD

Chapter Title

1   Eliot Framework for AI Self-Driving Cars

2   Crumbling Infrastructure and AI Self-Driving Cars

3   e-Billboarding and AI Self-Driving Cars

4   Kinship and AI Self-Driving Cars

5   Machine-Child Learning and AI Self-Driving Cars

6   Baby-on-Board and AI Self-Driving Car

7   Cop Car Chases and AI Self-Driving Cars

8   One-Shot Learning and AI Self-Driving Cars

This title is available via Amazon and other book sellers

Companion Book By This Author

Visionary Secrets of AI Driverless Cars

by Dr. Lance B. Eliot, MBA, PhD

Chapter Title

1   Eliot Framework for AI Self-Driving Cars

2   Seat Belts and AI Self-Driving Cars

3   Tiny EV's and AI Self-Driving Cars

4   Empathetic Computing and AI Self-Driving Cars

5   Ethics Global Variations and AI Self-Driving Cars

6   Computational Periscopy and AI Self-Driving Car

7   Superior Cognition and AI Self-Driving Cars

8   Amalgamating ODD's and AI Self-Driving Cars

This title is available via Amazon and other book sellers

Companion Book By This Author

Spearheading
AI Self-Driving Cars
by Dr. Lance B. Eliot, MBA, PhD

Chapter Title

1   Eliot Framework for AI Self-Driving Cars

2   Artificial Pain and AI Self-Driving Cars

3   Stop-and-Frisks and AI Self-Driving Cars

4   Cars Careening and AI Self-Driving Cars

5   Sounding Out Car Noises and AI Self-Driving Cars

6   No Speed Limit Autobahn and AI Self-Driving Car

7   Noble Cause Corruption and AI Self-Driving Cars

8   AI Rockstars and AI Self-Driving Cars

This title is available via Amazon and other book sellers

<u>Companion Book By This Author</u>

Spurring
AI Self-Driving Cars

by Dr. Lance B. Eliot, MBA, PhD

<u>Chapter Title</u>

1   Eliot Framework for AI Self-Driving Cars

2   Triune Brain Theory and AI Self-Driving Cars

3   Car Parts Thefts and AI Self-Driving Cars

4   Goto Fail Bug and AI Self-Driving Cars

5   Scrabble Understanding and AI Self-Driving Cars

6   Cognition Disorders and AI Self-Driving Car

7   Noise Pollution Abatement AI Self-Driving Cars

This title is available via Amazon and other book sellers

Companion Book By This Author

Avant-Garde
AI Driverless Cars

by Dr. Lance B. Eliot, MBA, PhD

Chapter Title

1   Eliot Framework for AI Self-Driving Cars

2   Linear Non-Threshold and AI Self-Driving Cars

3   Prediction Equation and AI Self-Driving Cars

4   Modular Autonomous Systems and AI Self-Driving Cars

5   Driver's Licensing and AI Self-Driving Cars

6   Offshoots and Spinoffs and AI Self-Driving Car

7   Depersonalization and AI Self-Driving Cars

This title is available via Amazon and other book sellers

<u>Companion Book By This Author</u>

AI Self-Driving Cars
Evolvement

by Dr. Lance B. Eliot, MBA, PhD

<u>Chapter Title</u>

1 Eliot Framework for AI Self-Driving Cars

2 Chief Safety Officers and AI Self-Driving Cars

3 Bounded Volumes and AI Self-Driving Cars

4 Micro-Movements Behaviors and AI Self-Driving Cars

5 Boeing 737 Aspects and AI Self-Driving Cars

6 Car Controls Commands and AI Self-Driving Car

7 Multi-Sensor Data Fusion and AI Self-Driving Cars

This title is available via Amazon and other book sellers

Companion Book By This Author

AI Driverless Cars
Chrysalis

by Dr. Lance B. Eliot, MBA, PhD

Chapter Title

1   Eliot Framework for AI Self-Driving Cars

2   Object Poses and AI Self-Driving Cars

3   Human In-The-Loop and AI Self-Driving Cars

4   Genius Shortage and AI Self-Driving Cars

5   Salvage Yards and AI Self-Driving Cars

6   Precision Scheduling and AI Self-Driving Car

7   Human Driving Extinction and AI Self-Driving Cars

This title is available via Amazon and other book sellers

Companion Book By This Author

Boosting
AI Autonomous Cars
by Dr. Lance B. Eliot, MBA, PhD

Chapter Title

1   Eliot Framework for AI Self-Driving Cars

2   Zero Knowledge Proofs and AI Self-Driving Cars

3   Active Shooter Response and AI Self-Driving Cars

4   Free Will and AI Self-Driving Cars

5   No Picture Yet of AI Self-Driving Cars

6   Boeing 737 Lessons and AI Self-Driving Cars

7   Preview Tesla FSD and AI Self-Driving Cars

8   LIDAR Industry and AI Self-Driving Cars

9   Uber IPO and AI Self-Driving Cars

10   Suing Automakers of AI Self-Driving Cars

11   Tesla Overarching FSD and AI Self-Driving Cars

12   Auto Repair Market and AI Self-Driving Cars

This title is available via Amazon and other book sellers

AI Self-Driving Cars Trendsetting

by Dr. Lance B. Eliot, MBA, PhD

Chapter Title

1   Eliot Framework for AI Self-Driving Cars

2   OTA Myths and AI Self-Driving Cars

3   Surveys and AI Self-Driving Cars

4   Tech Spies and AI Self-Driving Cars

5   Anxieties and AI Self-Driving Cars

6   Achilles Heel and AI Self-Driving Cars

7   Kids Alone and AI Self-Driving Cars

8   Infrastructure and AI Self-Driving Cars

9   Distracted Driving and AI Self-Driving Cars

10   Human Drivers and AI Self-Driving Cars

11   Anti-LIDAR Stance and AI Self-Driving Cars

12   Autopilot Team and AI Self-Driving Cars

13   Rigged Videos and AI Self-Driving Cars

14   Stalled Cars and AI Self-Driving Cars

15   Princeton Summit and AI Self-Driving Cars

16   Brittleness and AI Self-Driving Cars

17   Mergers and AI Self-Driving Cars

This title is available via Amazon and other book sellers

Companion Book By This Author

AI Autonomous Cars Forefront

by Dr. Lance B. Eliot, MBA, PhD

Chapter Title

1   Eliot Framework for AI Self-Driving Cars

2   Essential Stats and AI Self-Driving Cars

3   Stats Fallacies and AI Self-Driving Cars

4   Driver Bullies and AI Self-Driving Cars

5   Sunday Drives and AI Self-Driving Cars

6   Face Recog Bans and AI Self-Driving Cars

7   States On-The-Hook and AI Self-Driving Cars

8   Sensors Profiting and AI Self-Driving Cars

9   Unruly Riders and AI Self-Driving Cars

10   Father's Day and AI Self-Driving Cars

11   Summons Feature and AI Self-Driving Cars

12   Libra Cryptocurrency and AI Self-Driving Cars

13   Systems Naming and AI Self-Driving Cars

14   Mid-Traffic Rendezvous and AI Self-Driving Cars

15   Pairing Drones and AI Self-Driving Cars

16   Lost Wallet Study and AI Self-Driving Cars

This title is available via Amazon and other book sellers

Companion Book By This Author

AI Autonomous Cars Emergence

by Dr. Lance B. Eliot, MBA, PhD

Chapter Title

1   Eliot Framework for AI Self-Driving Cars

2   Dropping Off Riders and AI Self-Driving Cars

3   Add-On Kits Drive.AI and AI Self-Driving Cars

4   Boeing 737 Emergency Flaw and AI Self-Driving Cars

5   Spinout Tesla Autopilot and AI Self-Driving Cars

6   Earthquakes and AI Self-Driving Cars

7   Ford Mobility Lab and AI Self-Driving Cars

8   Apollo 11 Error Code and AI Self-Driving Cars

9   Nuro Self-Driving Vehicle and AI Self-Driving Cars

10   Safety First (SaFAD) Aptiv and AI Self-Driving Cars

11   Brainjacking Neuralink and AI Self-Driving Cars

12   Storming Area 51 and AI Self-Driving Cars

13   Riding Inside An AI Self-Driving Car

14   ACES Acronym and AI Self-Driving Cars

15   Kids Bike Riding and AI Self-Driving Cars

16   LIDAR Not Doomed and AI Self-Driving Cars

This title is available via Amazon and other book sellers

Companion Book By This Author

AI Autonomous Cars Progress

by Dr. Lance B. Eliot, MBA, PhD

Chapter Title

1 Eliot Framework for AI Self-Driving Cars

2 Risk-O-Meters and AI Self-Driving Cars

3 Eroding Car Devotion and AI Self-Driving Cars

4 Drunk Driving Rises With Smart Cars

5 Driver's Difficulties and Smart Cars

6 Millennials Aren't As Car Crazed As Baby Boomers

7 Risks Of AI Self-Driving Cars

8 Major Phase Shift and AI Self-Driving Cars

9 Level 3 Tech Misgivings For Smart Cars

10 Presidential Debate Lessons and AI Self-Driving Cars

11 Cloud Breeches and AI Self-Driving Cars

12 The Moral Imperative and AI Self-Driving Cars

13 Freed Up Driver Time And AI Self-Driving Car

14 Deadliest Highways and AI Self-Driving Cars

15 Your Lyin' Eyes and AI Self-Driving Cars

16 Elon Musk Physics Mindset and AI Self-Driving Cars

This title is available via Amazon and other book sellers

Companion Book By This Author

AI Self-Driving Cars
Prognosis

by Dr. Lance B. Eliot, MBA, PhD

Chapter Title

1   Eliot Framework for AI Self-Driving Cars

2   Roadkill and AI Self-Driving Cars

3   Safe Driver Cities and AI Self-Driving Cars

4   Tailgate Parties and AI Self-Driving Cars

5   Tesla's AI Chips and AI Self-Driving Cars

6   Elites-Only and AI Self-Driving Cars

7   Four Year Lifecycle and AI Self-Driving Cars

8   Entrepreneurs and AI Self-Driving Cars

9   Autopilot Crash Lessons and AI Self-Driving Cars

10 U.N. Framework and AI Self-Driving Cars

11 Sports Cars and AI Self-Driving Cars

12 Railroad Crossings and AI Self-Driving Cars

13 Robots That Drive and AI Self-Driving Car

14 Smarts Over Speed and AI Self-Driving Cars

15 Havoc Ratings and AI Self-Driving Cars

16 Sex-on-Wheels and AI Self-Driving Cars

This title is available via Amazon and other book sellers

Companion Book By This Author

AI Self-Driving Cars Momentum

by Dr. Lance B. Eliot, MBA, PhD

Chapter Title

1 Eliot Framework for AI Self-Driving Cars

2 Solving Loneliness and AI Self-Driving Cars

3 Headless Issues and AI Self-Driving Cars

4 Roaming Empty and AI Self-Driving Cars

5 Millennials Exodus and AI Self-Driving Cars

6 Recession Worries and AI Self-Driving Cars

7 Remote Operation Issues and AI Self-Driving Cars

8 Boomerang Kids and AI Self-Driving Cars

9 Waymo Coming To L.A. and AI Self-Driving Cars

10 Getting To Scale and AI Self-Driving Cars

11 Looking Alike and AI Self-Driving Cars

12 NOVA Documentary On AI Self-Driving Cars

13 Birthrate Changes and AI Self-Driving Cars

This title is available via Amazon and other book sellers

<u>Companion Book By This Author</u>

AI Self-Driving Cars
Headway

by Dr. Lance B. Eliot, MBA, PhD

<u>Chapter Title</u>

1   Eliot Framework for AI Self-Driving Cars

2   Germs Spreading and AI Self-Driving Cars

3   Carbon Footprint and AI Self-Driving Cars

4   Protestors Use Of AI Self-Driving Cars

5   Rogue Behavior and AI Self-Driving Cars

6   Using Human Drivers Versus AI Self-Driving Cars

7   Tesla Hodge-Podge On AI Self-Driving Cars

8   Solo Occupancy and AI Self-Driving Cars

9   Einstein's Twins Paradox and AI Self-Driving Cars

10   Nation-State Takeover Of AI Self-Driving Cars

11   Quantum Computers and AI Self-Driving Cars

12   Religious Revival And AI Self-Driving Cars

This title is available via Amazon and other book sellers

Companion Book By This Author

AI Self-Driving Cars
Vicissitude

by Dr. Lance B. Eliot, MBA, PhD

Chapter Title

1   Eliot Framework for AI Self-Driving Cars

2   Leaving A Tip and AI Self-Driving Cars

3   Digital Nudging and AI Self-Driving Cars

4   Carpool Lanes and AI Self-Driving Cars

5   Sleep Solving and AI Self-Driving Cars

6   Nostradamus and AI Self-Driving Cars

7   Advanced Driving and AI Self-Driving Cars

8   Cybertruck Windows Shattered Mystery

9   Artificial Stupidity and AI Self-Driving Cars

10   Revenue Estimates Of AI Self-Driving Cars

11 Survivalists and AI Self-Driving Cars

This title is available via Amazon and other book sellers

<u>Companion Book By This Author</u>

AI Self-Driving Cars
Autonomy

by Dr. Lance B. Eliot, MBA, PhD

<u>Chapter Title</u>

1   Eliot Framework for AI Self-Driving Cars

2   Your Bucket List and AI Self-Driving Cars

3   Highway Stunts and AI Self-Driving Cars

4   Future Wonderment and AI Self-Driving Cars

5   AI On-The-Fly Learning and AI Self-Driving Cars

6   Level 4 and Level 5 of AI Self-Driving Cars

7   Explaining Key Acronyms of AI Self-Driving Cars

8   Walmart Edge Computing and AI Self-Driving Cars

9   Stonehenge Lessons and AI Self-Driving Cars

10   Levels of Autonomy Feud and AI Self-Driving Cars

11 Hide and Escape Via AI Self-Driving Cars

This title is available via Amazon and other book sellers

Companion Book By This Author

AI Driverless Cars Transmutation

by Dr. Lance B. Eliot, MBA, PhD

Chapter Title

1   Eliot Framework for AI Self-Driving Cars

2   Backup Drivers and AI Self-Driving Cars

3   Teaching Kids about AI Self-Driving Cars

4   Hand-off Problem and AI Self-Driving Cars

5   Racial Bias and AI Self-Driving Cars

6   AI Consciousness and AI Self-Driving Cars

7   Machine Learning Riddles and AI Self-Driving Cars

8   Spurring Financial Literacy via AI Self-Driving Cars

9   GM Cruise Minivan and AI Self-Driving Cars

10   Car Off Cliff Lessons and AI Self-Driving Cars

11   Daughter Prank and AI Self-Driving Cars

This title is available via Amazon and other book sellers

<u>Companion Book By This Author</u>

AI Driverless Cars
Potentiality

by Dr. Lance B. Eliot, MBA, PhD

<u>Chapter Title</u>

1   Eliot Framework for AI Self-Driving Cars

2   Russian Values and AI Self-Driving Cars

3   Friendships Uplift and AI Self-Driving Cars

4   Dogs Driving and AI Self-Driving Cars

5   Hypodermic Needles and AI Self-Driving Cars

6   Sharing Self-Driving Tech Is Not Likely

7   Uber Driver "Kidnapper" Is Self-Driving Car Lesson

8   Gender Driving Biases In AI Self-Driving Cars

9   Slain Befriended Dolphins Are Self-Driving Car Lesson

10   Analysis Of AI In Government Report

11   Mobility Frenzy and AI Self-Driving Cars

This title is available via Amazon and other book sellers

Companion Book By This Author

AI Driverless Cars
Realities

by Dr. Lance B. Eliot, MBA, PhD

Chapter Title

1   Eliot Framework for AI Self-Driving Cars

2   Non-Driving Robots and AI Self-Driving Cars

3   HealthTech and AI Self-Driving Cars

4   Rudest Drivers and AI Self-Driving Cars

5   Aliens On Earth and AI Self-Driving Cars

6   AI Human Rights and AI Self-Driving Cars

7   Pope's AI Ethics and AI Self-Driving Cars

8   Human Judgment and AI Self-Driving Cars

9   DoD AI Ethics and AI Self-Driving Cars

10   Group Dynamics and AI Self-Driving Cars

11   Medical Emergencies Inside AI Self-Driving Cars

This title is available via Amazon and other book sellers

AI Self-Driving Cars
Materiality

by Dr. Lance B. Eliot, MBA, PhD

Chapter Title

1 Eliot Framework for AI Self-Driving Cars

2 Baby Sea Lion and AI Self-Driving Cars

3 Traffic Lights and AI Self-Driving Cars

4 Roadway Edge Computing and AI Self-Driving Cars

5 Ground Penetrating Radar and AI Self-Driving Cars

6 Upstream Parable and AI Self-Driving Cars

7 Red-Light Auto-Stopping and Self-Driving Cars

8 Falseness of Superhuman AI Self-Driving Cars

9 Social Distancing and AI Self-Driving Cars

10 Apollo 13 Lessons and AI Self-Driving Cars

11 FutureLaw and AI Self-Driving Cars

ABOUT THE AUTHOR

Dr. Lance B. Eliot, Ph.D., MBA is a globally recognized AI expert and thought leader, an experienced executive and leader, a successful serial entrepreneur, and a noted scholar on AI, including that his Forbes and AI Trends columns have amassed over 2.8+ million views, his books on AI are frequently ranked in the Top 10 of all-time AI books, his journal articles are widely cited, and he has developed and fielded dozens of AI systems.

He currently serves as the CEO of Techbruim, Inc. and has over twenty years of industry experience including serving as a corporate officer in billion-dollar sized firms and was a partner in a major consulting firm. He is also a successful entrepreneur having founded, ran, and sold several high-tech related businesses.

Dr. Eliot previously hosted the popular radio show *Technotrends* that was also available on American Airlines flights via their in-flight audio program, he has made appearances on CNN, has been a frequent speaker at industry conferences, and his podcasts have been downloaded over 100,000 times.

A former professor at the University of Southern California (USC), he founded and led an innovative research lab on Artificial Intelligence. He also previously served on the faculty of the University of California Los Angeles (UCLA) and was a visiting professor at other major universities. He was elected to the International Board of the Society for Information Management (SIM), a prestigious association of over 3,000 high-tech executives worldwide.

He has performed extensive community service, including serving as Senior Science Adviser to the Congressional Vice-Chair of the Congressional Committee on Science & Technology. He has served on the Board of the OC Science & Engineering Fair (OCSEF), where he is also has been a Grand Sweepstakes judge, and likewise served as a judge for the Intel International SEF (ISEF). He served as the Vice-Chair of the Association for Computing Machinery (ACM) Chapter, a prestigious association of computer scientists. Dr. Eliot has been a shark tank judge for the USC Mark Stevens Center for Innovation on start-up pitch competitions and served as a mentor for several incubators and accelerators in Silicon Valley and in Silicon Beach.

Dr. Eliot holds a Ph.D. from USC, MBA, and Bachelor's in Computer Science, and earned the CDP, CCP, CSP, CDE, and CISA certifications.

ADDENDUM

AI Self-Driving Cars Materiality

Practical Advances in Artificial Intelligence (AI) and Machine Learning

By
Dr. Lance B. Eliot, MBA, PhD

———

For supplemental materials of this book, visit:
www.ai-selfdriving-cars.guru

For special orders of this book, contact:
LBE Press Publishing
Email: LBE.Press.Publishing@gmail.com